JOSEPH CONRAD

In the same series:

(continued on page 126)

MODERN LITERATURE MONOGRAPHS
GENERAL EDITOR: Lina Mainiero

JOSEPH CONRAD

Martin Tucker

FREDERICK UNGAR PUBLISHING CO.

75-1610

Copyright © 1976 by Frederick Ungar Publishing Co., Inc.
Printed in the United States of America
Designed by Anita Duncan

Library of Congress Cataloging in Publication Data

Tucker, Martin.
    Joseph Conrad.

    (Modern literature monographs)
    Biliography: p.
    Includes index.
    1. Conrad, Joseph, 1857–1924—Criticism and inter-
pretation.
PR6005.04Z887   823'.9'12   75-37265
ISBN 0–8044–2928–6

Contents

Chronology

1857	Conrad is born at Berdiczew in Russian-occupied Poland on 3 December. He is christened Jozef Teodor Konrad Nalecz Korzeniowski.
1862	Conrad's father Apollo Nalecz Korzeniowski is sentenced to penal exile in Siberia by the Czarist Russian government for helping to organize the secret Polish National Committee. Conrad's mother petitions to go with her husband, and takes their only child (Conrad) with her.
1865	Conrad's mother dies. Conrad's maternal uncle, Tadeusz Bobrowski, takes responsibility for care of Conrad.
1868	Father allowed to return from exile to Lemberg, Galicia. Conrad joins him.
1869	Conrad and father move to Cracow. Conrad's father dies 23 May.
1870	Conrad's grandmother appointed his guardian. Conrad's education supervised by a tutor from University of Cracow.
1874–78	Conrad leaves Poland 14 October for France. He serves on French ships in voyages to the West Indies and Central America. He meets Dominic Cervoni who becomes the model for Jean Peyrol, "an old Dominic" in *The Rover*; for Nostromo in *Nostromo*; for Attilio in *Suspense*; and possibly for certain aspects of Tom Lingard in *Almayer's Folly*, *An Outcast of the Islands*, and *The Rescue*. Cervoni is used under his own name in Conrad's

fessional writer. Begins association with *Blackwood's* magazine.

1898   *Tales of Unrest* appears. Son Borys born. Conrad and family move to Kent.

1901   Writes *Typhoon,* and begins *Romance* with Ford Madox (Hueffer) Ford as collaborator. Ends his association with Blackwood's.

1903–04   Writes *Nostromo* at Pent Farm in Kent.

1905   Travels to Europe for four months. Writes "Autocracy and War" (in *Notes on Life and Letters*). Writes two chapters of *The Mirror of the Sea* and begins *The Secret Agent.*

1906   John Alexander, second son, born in London 2 August. Conrad visits France.

1907   Children ill in France. Conrad takes them to Geneva for treatment. Writes *Chance.*

1908   Begins *Razumov* (in revised title, *Under Western Eyes*).

1909   Writes "The Secret Sharer," and continues work on *Under Western Eyes.*

1911–12   Finishes *Chance.*

1913–14   Works on *Victory.*

1914   Returns with family to Poland; with outbreak of World War I, they are stranded there. Arrangements made to return them to England.

1915   Writes "Poland Revisited" (in *Notes on Life and Letters*) as series of four articles for *Daily Mail.*

1916   Begins rewriting *The Rescue,* on which he had stopped work 20 years before, on advice of his friend and agent J. B. Pinker. Advises the Admiralty on naval craft in North Sea.

1917–18   Writes *The Arrow of Gold.* Writes prefaces for a forthcoming collected edition.

1919   Moves to Oswalds, Bishopbourne, near Canterbury.

1920   Dramatizes *The Secret Agent*.

1921   Works on "Suspense" in Corsica. Begins *The Rover*.

1922   *The Secret Agent* in dramatic form is commercial failure. London run is brief. Conrad finishes *The Rover*.

1923   Conrad makes first voyage to United States. His sojourns in New York and Boston are great personal triumphs.

1924   Conrad declines offer of knighthood. He dies 3 August of a heart attack. He is buried in Canterbury.

1

Conrad's Truths: An Introduction

Joseph Conrad, whose greatest work portrays the crises of identity of men and women in isolation from their society, was at home with the traditions of three countries to which he could give his allegiance: Poland, where he was born on December 6, 1857, as Jozef Teodor Konrad Nalecz Korzeniowski, in the Russian-occupied Polish Ukraine; France, the country he idealized for its sense of form and order, and in which he lived from 1874 to 1878; and England, of which he became a naturalized citizen in 1886. Because of his self-imposed exile and his new allegiances, he was compelled to draw to his fullest depth the complex, arbitrary, and ambiguous processes by which men and women come to terms with themselves. In creating his fiction he recreated his agony. Through his painful journeys, couched in symbolic and metaphoric language, he presented to the reader the stages by which some men and women reached integration or re-integration, and some did not.

All his life he was a temperamental agnostic. He could state facts clearly and simply, but for him this was not the truth of the matter, the whole of his story. He was frightened of absolutes, of their capability of unbalancing the world through the weight of their rigid doctrine. Yet he was also searching for a hierarchy of moral guidance. He wanted a fluid association of principles as his rule of conduct. Yet he was fearful of anarchy and lack of discipline. Caught in the dilemma between these two extremes of human behavior, tyranny and anarchy, he struggled to find a middle base.

Conrad's ambivalence—in the search for absolutes and the disavowal of them in the belief that no proof exists as yet of their truth—is reflected in an endless number of ways in his work and life. Conrad's youth reveals his attraction to the impulsive and the ordered, to paralysis and high-strung abandon. When he was a child in Poland, his guardian uncle, Tadeusz Bobrowski, warned him to curb his romantic excesses and flights of dream. Conrad's decision at seventeen to take on a career at sea was evolved, at least partly, from a romantic notion of the freedom of the sea. His uncle, who at first opposed the move and then reluctantly gave his consent, warned Conrad of the dangers of an undisciplined nature and of the need for firm moral guidelines. Shortly after Conrad arrived in Marseilles in 1874, he became a gun-runner for the Spanish Carlist cause (the followers of the deposed Spanish monarch ran their operations from across the border); he had a romantic liaison with a lady of some notoriety; he saw the two-masted sailing ship, the purchase of which was partly financed by the money his uncle had sent him for living expenses, wrecked; he gambled in the casinos; and he suffered a serious, self-inflicted wound. His French interlude concluded with a visit from his uncle, who both chastized and tended him. Conrad turned then to the British merchant marine. Although he seems to have been a man of sober mood from this time on, vestiges of his romantic nature continued to surface. He was a dandy in dress. He remained mysteriously aloof from his sea companions. Even in the Far East, Conrad showed his recklessness and restlessness; he gave up jobs, without much visible reason for his actions, though he had no other means of support.

Conrad's personality—which some critics have called "evasive" because of his refusal to make simple conclusions about character and situation in his work—may be traced to his childhood experiences, the bitter drama he witnessed in Siberia as his mother lay dying and his father was broken in health and spirit. Apollo Korzeniowski, Conrad's father, who protested Russian autocracy and subjugation, was arrested in 1861 and exiled to the Vologda region of northern Russia. Conrad's mother elected to go with her husband into penal servitude and took the three-year-old Conrad with her. When Conrad's mother, suffering from tuberculosis, petitioned the Russian authorities to allow her and the child to return to Poland, her request was denied.

Conrad, who watched the drama, who saw his mother die and his father deteriorate from a handsome, bold, romantic thinker, playwright and patriot to a feeble, gray-haired man, must have wondered at the absurdity and awesomeness of tyranny. Although some years later Apollo Korzeniowski was paid public tribute and memorialized for his patriotic sacrifices, Conrad was never able to overcome his own sense of futility at his father's romantic, rebellious gesture. He was, alternately, drawn to it by a spirit of love and respect.

Conrad drew upon rebels like his father for his heroes. Such men commit the most consequential acts of their lives out of an overwhelming impulse. They spend the rest of their lives paying the consequences of that impulse. In Conrad's novels the impulse is often to revolution. Initially, the motion and seeming vitality attracts the hero. Conrad is careful, however, to show that the initial attraction is illusory. The revolutionists in his novels more often than not are exposed as shallow, corrupt, foolish, and exploitative. Conrad's definition of revolution was "a short cut in the rational development of national needs in response to the growth of worldwide ideals." By "short cut" he meant a lack of orderly continuity in the scheme of the universe, whether that break in continuity came from the effort to jump ahead or to keep back change.

The rebel, the outcast, the man of isolation, the hero in an indifferent or hostile society—these are part of the Conradian complex of characters. Many of them are young but not all. What they have in common is a sense of apartness from their companions. Even when they succeed in a task that involves the cooperation of other men, they still possess a quality of aloneness. This quality of aloneness is more marked in Conrad's heroes than in his villains.

In Conrad's work, a third party, in addition to the hero and villain, is celebrated: he is the narrator. Marlow, who tells Jim's story in Lord Jim, is "one of us," one of "we sailors." In Victory the agent who brings food and means of protection (though too late for Heyst) is Davidson of the Sissie, another of the society of sailors who provide solidarity and shelter to wandering, isolated men. In Conrad's fiction, this pairing—the isolated man and the social man, the one ill at ease with his society and the man adjusted to his way of life—often occurs. The narrator, the seemingly well-adjusted man, the figure of moderate success and average good will, becomes fascinated with a creature who is intriguing because of his apartness from society.

Conrad's recurrent combination of the isolated man (the subject of overt scrutiny) and the conventional man (the narrator who reveals himself by his peculiar way of observing things) suggests that Conrad believed the "whole story" lay in the recollection of character in the midst of action. This recollection was supplied by a narrator in his review of past events. Conrad also insisted on a sense of the fluidity of time—

past and present intermingling and affecting each other so that the actor in the story, and the reader of the story, cannot stop to consider judgment until the "whole story" has been cast forth.

These qualities in Conrad's work, and in his personality, give precedence to indirect suggestion over overt statement, and make of time a tournament with memory. Those critics who call Conrad "evasive" often refer to these qualities. The evasiveness, however, is that of a man fearful that moral absolutes and laws, with the unwitting help of his fiction, will be proclaimed prematurely.

Conrad came to writing late: he was thirty-two years old when he began to write his first novel, *Almayer's Folly*. He had been a merchant seaman in the British maritime service since he shipped aboard *The Skimmer of the Sea* on July 11, 1878. One morning, in 1889, as he liked to tell it, he finished breakfast in his London boarding house, and simply began to write the first page. The pen moved itself. Undoubtedly, Conrad had been thinking about the novel and about his possible career as writer for some time. But Conrad's version of the occasion shows his predilection—perhaps his need—to symbolize all occasions. For Conrad, the act had to be *fated*. There had to be preparations. (Conrad is fond of seemingly irrelevant details as ritualistic vestments of inevitability.) But if Conrad was obsessed with a sense of the inevitability of things, he also saw life rationally. He knew the beginnings of a journey—in his case the writing expedition—could not predict the middle and end of that journey. Its itinerary could not be predicted till the journey was lived through and experienced. Conrad then was probably not surprised that it took him five years to finish his first novel, nor that he continued to fear the risks and insecurities of a professional writer's life even after he had committed himself to the goal of becoming a professional writer.

The need for alternatives—pronounced in Conrad —exhibits itself in three events in Conrad's early life. Conrad did not begin to write until he had his merchant seaman's papers: once he had established himself into a settled profession he could try his skill in a more hazardous trade. Conrad obtained his merchant seaman's papers in the same year as his citizenship papers. Now he felt free to journey to strange places because he had established a new home base. Conrad must have admired, even if he had not consciously planned, these neat, tidy confluences of events. All the pieces of his life seemed to be flowing together.

For a long time Conrad wavered between the sea as a way of life and literature as a profession. In 1890, while he was commanding a Belgian steamer on the Congo river, he contracted a tropical disease from which he suffered for several years. In spite of ill health, he continued his maritime service until 1894. In 1895 he published his first novel, *Almayer's Folly*, which proved moderately successful. Encouraged by his publisher to continue in the same path, Conrad wrote *An Outcast of the Islands* the following year.

Conrad's decision to give up the sea may have been spurred by his marriage to Jessie George, three weeks after the publication of his second novel. It has been pointed out by Conrad's biographers that during his courtship of Jessie, Conrad told her of his fears of an imminent death: "he prefaced his proposal with the announcement 'that he had not very long to live and no intention of having children.'" Some critics, Thomas Moser and Albert Guerard among them, see Conrad's late marriage and his mordant view preceding it— "when Jessie George accepted him, his face wore an 'expression of acute suffering'"—as reflective of a fearful ambivalence. These critics posit Conrad as a man desperately afraid of sex, impotence, and women, and desperately desiring the shield of maternal armor. Other biographers see in Conrad's late marriage simply the act of a sensitive man who did not wish to involve himself in marital responsibilities until he felt able to handle them.

In spite of Conrad's fears, the marriage with Jessie George proved a long and happy one. She provided him with the stability of a regular household and constant companionship, and she ministered to his periodic attacks of anxiety and terror.

Although he made several tentative attempts to return to the sea between 1895 and 1900, Conrad was committing himself to the sedentary and risky life of a professional writer. He wrote the stories that would be issued in his first collection, *Tales of Unrest*, and he began the composition of his first short masterpiece, *The Nigger of the Narcissus*.

Conrad's career as writer was one fraught with all the insecurity of that hazardous trade. He was critically acclaimed, but he was not a popular writer. He never earned, until 1913, an income with which he and his family might feel comfortable. Indeed, in 1902 his first publisher, Blackwood's, who had encouraged and supported him, broke with him. Mr. Blackwood felt the company could no longer suffer the loss that publication of Conrad's books entailed. Conrad found another publisher, but he remained in debt for some time. Then, in 1913, with the publication of *Chance*, he became a popular success. At the same time, his work declined in quality.

In 1914 Conrad and his family made their first visit to Poland since he had left it as a young man. War broke out within a month after their arrival, and Conrad and his family were briefly in danger of being forced to spend the remainder of the war in a land ruled by a government Conrad had criticized severely. Inter-

national dignitaries arranged for the transfer of the
family to Austria, and then to England. This experience
impressed Conrad so much that he dedicated *The Rescue*, published in 1920, to Frederick Courtlandt Pen-
field, "Last Ambassador of the United States of America to the Late Austrian Empire." The general good
will Conrad derived from the experience was as important as the immediate aid of transport. It became for
him an instance of the esteem in which he was held in
the Western world.

This sense of good will, of a ripening mellowness,
is evident in Conrad's work from "The Shadow-Line,"
published in 1917. In that story of passing over the line
from insecurity and fear to self-confidence and acceptance of responsibility, Conrad relinquished his
armor of irony. The works that follow are characterized
by a willingness to leave, unquestioned, romantic notions about man's behavior. The ironist became a
sentimentalist.

In this last period of his life, Conrad completed
four novels, a fragment of a fifth, and several short
stories. Ever the conscientious craftsman, he kept up
with his habits of self-discipline even when his health
was poor. His writings during this period show a strong
debt to autobiographical experience, nothing new in
Conrad, but the writings consist mainly of revisions
and/or completions of manuscripts and notes left over
from earlier years.

During this time Conrad suffered from ill health,
particularly in the increasing severity of attacks of gout.
He also undertook a new method of writing, dictation,
a method that no doubt eased the physical chore of
writing but led to self-consciousness, and inhibition of
expression. Yet the decline in Conrad's literary powers
cannot alone be attributed to poor health. In Conrad's
earlier years he was afflicted with illness and nervous
strain, and, as his letters attest, periodic bouts with

"sterility" of inspiration; indeed it was an incapacitating illness contracted during his voyage into the Congo that led him to give up the sea and begin writing. All during those early years he was beset with financial, personal, and physical problems. Perhaps a more apt perception is that, after the immense agonies of creative work that produced the masterpieces of his early and middle years, he felt a spiritual depletion, a sense of emptiness (though it is wise to remember that Conrad often spoke, from the beginning of his literary career, about a sense of emptiness; in his letters he used the French phrase "la sensation du vide").

Conrad's last years were in marked contrast to his early ones. Successful, respected, a recognized literary giant, he was the dispenser of advice to young writers and the model of stature for others. He was offered a knighthood in 1924 but refused the honor. He traveled to many places, receiving acclaim throughout the world; his first and only trip to the United States in 1923 was a great personal triumph. Perhaps his last works were lacking in the tension of his earlier and middle periods, because he had conquered his obstacles, scaled his heights, and come through. He had, in any case, made peace with his demons. He died on August 3, 1924, after suffering a heart seizure.

Conrad published several memoirs—*The Mirror of the Sea* in 1906, *A Personal Record* (also published as *Some Reminiscences*) in 1912, and *Notes on Life and Letters* in 1921. "Autocracy and War," written in 1905 and "Poland Revisited," written after his visit in 1914, are among his most famous essays. His novels and short stories remain, however, his most revealing work, and which he personally felt were most important.

Conrad's comments on his novels have received wide attention. His prolific letter-writing, in which he comments on his craft and the "terrors" of that discipline, often provide valuable insight into his intentions. Yet it is also true that Conrad in the course of years changed his "facts" and assertions: he often retold in different guises the quicksilver inspirations that prompted his insights. If he were caught up in the face of a fact he had forgotten or twisted out of shape, he was able to dismiss his act with the notion of "the truth of my sensations." An example often given of Conrad's penchant for the "truth," as opposed to the "fact" of something (or what one critic calls the willful inaccuracy of Conrad's memory about his works and life) is a story told by R. L. Mégroz about a conversation between Conrad and his wife Jessie. "On one of his naughty days he said that 'The Black Mate' was his first work, and when I [Jessie] said, 'No, *Almayer's Folly* was the first thing you ever did,' he burst out: 'If I like to say "The Black Mate" was my first work, I shall say so.'"

The "truth of my own sensations," a phrase Conrad uses in his Author's Note to *Within the Tides* is a philosophic issue in which sensations may be taken to mean all knowledge revealed through the imagination and senses. Conrad's view is that truth is elusive, always one step higher or deeper than its partial appearance in the form of facts. In Conrad the truth, or the "whole story," must be reconstructed from the partial views of each of the narrator-observers. The truth, or the "whole story," is not a matter only of what is being seen, but who is seeing it, how he sees it, and why he sees it through his peculiar vision.

In his preface to *The Nigger of the Narcissus* Conrad said, "My task which I am trying to achieve is, by the power of the written word to make you hear, to make you feel—it is, before all, to make you *see*. That —and no more, and it is everything. If I succeed, you shall find there according to your deserts: encouragement, consolation, fear, charm—all you demand—and, perhaps, also that glimpse of truth for which you have forgotten to ask."

Conrad was particularly attracted to the visual. The dominance of the visual image is intimately connected with Conrad's reliance on the technique of point of view. Conrad came to believe that viewpoint, the vision limited by character and background, was the only way in which truth could be apprehended.

This use of the visual, and of the technique of point of view, is not a formula Conrad rigidly developed. He was a craftsman who constantly revised and reshaped his work to suit his discoveries of observation and technique. His comments in the Author's Notes to the *Collected Edition* are stated in informal, impressionistic language. Indeed, Conrad wrote about his fear of entrapment in any rules, whether for living or for writing, since the dogma of tyranny was as much anathema to him as the upheaval of anarchy. Conrad was always aware of the limitations of man's vision. Yet he was also aware that man must act despite his limited knowledge.

Thus, in Conrad's work, there is the pervading sense of futility that comes from the despair that one will quickly reach the boundaries of his limited knowledge. The truth, that is, the whole truth, Conrad tells his readers, is a tantalizing myth. But, as Conrad proved with his novels, one can get closer to it. That, finally, is what man can achieve. For Conrad, it is enough.

2

Paralysis and Freedom: *Lord Jim*

Lord Jim, Conrad's third novel to be published, heralds his emergence as a force in modern British literature not to be ignored.

Because *Lord Jim* deals with the psychic—some would call it the symbolic—journey of character on which the literal journey of plot sequence is superimposed, Conrad chose a technique that constantly suggests an altering order of consciousness. In choosing this difficult (but now very modern) technique—that is, a story told from the developing awareness of its narrators—Conrad has annoyed some critics who want a story plain. Most notable among these may be E. M. Forster, who has always insisted that a novel must have a story. Forster found Conrad's voyaging into the veils of time and awareness a dodge among shadows of ideas. Conrad's achievement in *Lord Jim* may be debatable, but to deny him the right to the tools of his own making is to make of the writer's trade a closed port.

There is, of course, story in *Lord Jim*, a great deal of it, and the reader can restructure the events into a chronological sequence in order to see it "plain." However, it is essential to see the story, finally, in the way Conrad saw it—that is, as a series of insights on the part of a moderate man, Marlow, into the nature of the endlessly fascinating character of an eccentric romantic, Lord Jim.

Marlow's journey of awareness carries him from his first glimpse of Jim in a courtroom, where Jim is being tried for desertion of his ship, to the moment of Jim's death in Patusan. Marlow is a more conventional character than Jim, and part of Jim's appeal to Marlow is the glamor that comes from Jim's strangeness and Jim's alienation from his peers. Yet Marlow, like Jim, also harbors a need to dive into the murky waters of psychic understanding. Marlow moderates his need, controls it by using Jim as his vicarious experience, and grows to love Jim as a brother, as a double who has done the things he, Marlow, cannot do.

Conrad apparently felt that even such a moderate and rational man as Marlow, a man imbued with common sense, could not provide the whole story. He thus presents in the first four chapters another narrator, a nameless story-teller who may be said to set an "objective" tone before the subjective view of Marlow takes over. This narrator presents the story of Jim from the outside—Jim as a strange, haunted creature after his disgrace, and Jim in two earlier episodes in his life. Jim is fascinating also to this first narrator, but not in the profound way he is to Marlow.

The nameless narrator begins the novel with a description of the fallen man Jim, but the reader will not know until the third chapter the facts of that "fall." He will know only that Jim, in his inability to forgive himself his one moment of cowardice and move along to a new career and life, excites the interest of many of his observers. He will learn that Jim, a man who once swore never to forsake his duty, has become a wanderer over the Eastern face of the earth, unable to face anyone who recognizes him as the officer who deserted a sinking ship. Later, Marlow will suggest the low state of Jim—his reputation and his own judgment as society's outcast—by a device known in the twentieth century as guilt by association: two men, Chester and Captain

Robinson, offer to hire Jim as "caretaker" of bird excrement on a desert island. (It is important to remember that Jim has been described as "clean," well-scrubbed, and virtuous—the very model of a blond, blue-eyed, slim and immaculate British youth—in his days of innocence.)

The nameless narrator brings the reader to the courtroom where the *Patna* case is being heard, and where Jim stands as one of three defendants (the other officers have fled). It is at this point that Marlow takes over the story, and begins his own odyssey of understanding.

Some narrative facts emerge clearly and in conventional time sequence from the first narrator's account. Briefly, the narrative facts are these: the ship *Patna* has collided with a wreck in the dark of night. The ship's officers, aware they had failed to observe safety regulations by stowing too few lifeboats aboard, decided to desert the ship without awakening the 800 passengers bound for Mecca on a pilgrimage. Standing in the midst of the sleeping pilgrims, Jim, a junior officer who had no knowledge of his superior officers' premeditated violation of safety regulations, is startled by one of the pilgrims who awakens and demands water. Envisioning the panic that will occur when the other pilgrims awaken, Jim decides to jump into one of the lifeboats. Jim has thus committed an act that all his training and background have taught him is reprehensible.

Instead of sinking, however, the *Patna* is rescued by a passing ship, whose commander, a French lieutenant, risks his life to board the *Patna* and direct it to port. All the pilgrims are saved. Jim and the officers do not know of the ship's happy fate. The captain of the *Patna*, one of the first to desert, discovers the turn of events shortly after he has landed on shore. He lies to the authorities in the hope of implicating his officers and absolving himself of responsibility. A court inquiry is ordered. While the other officers disappear, Jim stays to suffer his trial and punishment.

The court strips Jim of his marine officer's certification. Jim now takes one job after another—he pleases his employers, but he cannot bear to stay in any one place long enough to be spotted as a deserter of the *Patna*. Marlow, who has brooded about the youth since his first meeting with him, seeks to find a home for Jim. He encourages the wealthy German trader, Stein, to send Jim to Patusan, a settlement on the east coast of Borneo which Stein owns. Here Jim will be isolated from the world of the *Patna* and from his shame. Here he will have his second chance.

Stein's words of advice to the young man are, "In the destructive element immerse,"—advice that summarizes one of the themes in the novel. For Stein recognizes in Jim the dreamer and idealist who is bound for worldly defeat unless he learns how to handle the "destructive element"—the real world of ugly facts and brutal men.

Jim arrives in Patusan to assume the duties of another of Stein's protégés, Cornelius, who has been demoted to serve as Jim's assistant. Resentful of Jim, Cornelius makes veiled threats to him. Jim ignores Cornelius's petty bickerings and concentrates on his major goal—ridding the island of rebellious, terrorist natives. He raids and destroys the camp of the brutal Sherif Ali. He reinstates to power Doramin and his son Dain Waris, who had been ousted from their legitimate princely authority by rebels. He is accorded the title Tuan (Malay, for Lord) by a grateful and loving people.

At this point Gentleman Jim Brown and his gang arrive at Patusan. Conrad has Marlow say that Brown may have come for supplies, he may have been curious about the stories he heard about this ideal gentleman

Tuan Jim, or he may simply have seen the name Patusan on a map. In any case, Brown shows up, as Conrad
implies he is bound to do. Brown and his gang plunder
the island until Jim and Dain Waris, the Crown Prince
of Patusan, surround them. At this point Brown and his
gang can easily be captured, though not without blood-
shed. Jim—for reasons that remain unclear, because
Marlow can only speculate on Jim's motivations and
actions, and Marlow is telling the story—offers Gentleman Brown safe passage out of Patusan. The offer is
generous, but Brown rejects it. With the aid of the
treacherous Cornelius, Brown and his gang escape in
the dead of night from their encirclement and sneak
into the unsuspecting camp of Dain Waris, where they
murder the Crown Prince and most of his soldiers. The
motivations for Brown's massacre are also left as speculations, except that Conrad makes it evident that all
that happens seems inevitable, a part of the progress of
a morality play.

Jim, who accepts responsibility for Dain Waris's
death, now must choose from several alternatives: he
can overcome Brown and rid the island of the alien,
evil presence of Brown's gang; he can flee with Cornelius's daughter, Jewel, who has become his mistress;
he can surrender to Brown, and admit total collapse of
his dream of a better world on Patusan, or he can
choose to suffer just punishment for his act of generosity, a generosity that made it possible for Brown to
gain time, regroup his gang and steal up on an unsuspecting opposition. In choosing the last alternative, Jim
walks into the royal camp of Doramin. Doramin, who
has loved and revered Jim, raises his pistol and shoots
him in the heart. Doramin has taken the life of the man
responsible for his son's death.

The second part of *Lord Jim*—the journey to
Patusan and Jim's redemption there—is demonstrably
less impressive than the accounting of Jim's impulsive

moment of cowardice and his flight from shame. Yet the second part is a necessary component of Jim's story. Were *Lord Jim* to end with Jim's restless pursuit over the Eastern world, the novel would be a story of Jim's decline, just as Conrad's first two novels *Almayer's Folly* and *An Outcast of the Islands* were stories of decline. Without Patusan, Jim would be another self-pitying, failed idealist. Conrad's Jim is a man who captures his second chance.

In *Heart of Darkness*, a work that is intimately connected with *Lord Jim* since they were written concurrently and use similar methods of narrative, Conrad spoke of the "fascination of the abominable." Jim is, of course, not abominable, but he is "impossible" and "confounded," because he will not act like other people. He has committed a crime, but he does not take the easy way out when opportunities present themselves. The other officers of the *Patna*, for example, either lie or run away; Jim stays willingly, though his "judge" wishes he would flee. It is this fascination of the "abominable"—that is, fascination with a man who is both criminal and saint—that impels the action and gives the novel its moral focus.

The real story of *Lord Jim* then is the meaning Jim's life holds for his observers. In trying to understand him each is trying to understand his own potentialities for disorder in the hope that such illumination will control their impulse and drift to disorder.

Among these observers are the nameless narrator, Marlow, Brierly, the French lieutenant who rescues the *Patna*, Stein, and Gentleman Jim Brown.

The nameless narrator, in introducing Jim, describes him as possessing "exquisite sensibility." The narrator also relays the information that many of Jim's employers call him "confounded fool!" Immediately then the conflicting views of Jim are set forth. An incident at the end of the first chapter provides an example of the distance between Jim's ideals and his conduct. The narrator tells of the time when Jim, then a trainee aboard his ship, saw a man struggling in the waters below. Characteristically, Jim thinks of what he should do, then makes his decision to jump into the water to rescue the man. The captain of the ship, however, restrains him, pointing out that someone else has already jumped into the water. The captain's words to Jim are: "Too late, youngster."

In short, Jim does not seek the "normal" pleasures; he quests after heroic action, but some psychic inhibition restrains him from his pursuit. After the rescue of the drowning man, everyone but Jim celebrates the occasion. Jim broods alone, determined to find a way to shine so brilliantly that others will think of him as a young man superior in quality to other men.

The nameless narrator also describes an accident in Jim's life before his desertion of the *Patna* that takes on the quality of a symbolic portrait. Struck by a spar in a storm, Jim is obliged to leave his ship as it enters port, and go to the hospital. In his hospital bed, he suffers an agony of depression. He thinks vaguely of leaving the sea. He feels alienated from the other seamen in the hospital. Finally, the depression lifts, and he goes back to his ship.

This episode, along with Jim's failure to act *immediately* in saving a drowning man, indicate that Jim is not, as the outside view would suggest, a self-confident man. Jim is, from the beginning, an isolated man. Because of his youth and background, and his conventional good looks, that isolation is less evident to the public eye.

Jim's accident, which results in his hospitalization, is significant in another way. Jim always aims for the top of the ladder: he does not, until the end of his life, allow himself to wander into the center of things. After his disgrace, he does not seek inwardly for resources, but runs on a mechanical track of flight, always on the same surface. Conrad is suggesting in the symbolic structure of Jim's fall and triumph (that is, his courage to accept responsibility for a mistake he has made, and for his own death) an overarching ambition; a plummet into the depths of depression when Jim believes himself incapable of rising and shining above other men; to his redemption when he is able to accept his errors without losing faith in himself. At the beginning of the novel, Jim craves exaltation and is struck down; at the end, he has put himself in a circle of men and forgiven those who have wounded him, has even forgiven the man who kills him. The symbolism of the bullet entering Jim's heart, in the middle of his body, is also pertinent. Jim is no longer associated with exalted heights or abysmal depths.

Marlow, in the narration of his recollections, says that Jim came from the right place: he was "one of us." Marlow describes Jim as the offspring of parents not clever or amusing, whose life style is founded on honest faith and the courage to look temptation straight in the face and reject it. Such people, Marlow continues, are unintellectual, unpretentious, and possess an "unthinking and blessed stiffness before the outward and inward terrors, before the sight of nature, and the seductive corruption of men." Ideas do not seduce them.

Marlow says of Jim: "he was outwardly so typical of that good, stupid kind we like to feel marching right and left of us in life, of the kind that is not disturbed by the vagaries of intelligence and the perversions of—of nerves, let us say." There seems no doubt Conrad admired common sense and the disciplined working man, and that he understood the tragic irony of the fact that ideas do vitiate men. When Conrad spoke of the perversions of "nerves" and the power of resistance to corruption that comes from being "unintellectual," he was not, however, condemning intellectuals nor handing a laurel to insular philistines. He was describing a fact of the human condition. Conrad knew the pain, the "vitiation," that ideas bring—such a visitation is a curse, but a magnificent experience, and those "cursed" with it must, like Prometheus, suffer their gifts. In Conrad's novels, characters who are not moved by the "perversions of nerves" to agonies of conscience and indecision survive, while characters who are plagued with unconventional ideas (and who may act on them) suffer torment and death.

Some readers may argue that Jim lives in a world of illusion—he lives by a code which most people only subscribe to on public occasions. Yet Conrad's simpler people may also be living in a world of illusion, the illusion that they can get through life without facing "ideas" or looking into things. Marlow says, "Hang ideas! They are tramps, vagabonds, knocking at the back door of your mind, each taking a little of your substance, each carrying away some crumb of that belief in a few simple notions you must cling to if you want to live decently and would like to die easy!"

At the point at which Marlow is rendering his narrative, he is an older man, mature in his share of experience. He is looking back on a series of events, the significance of which he did not quite understand at the time they occurred. He reveals that he always harbored the feeling of an older, sympathetic brother to the young man Jim who had not yet found himself. Marlow is somewhat sentimental about Jim, and about all the "sea-puppies" he has helped to train and guide through life. He feels satisfied in the knowledge that he has provided direction for young seamen, and he expresses his gratitude for the memory of young men who, having trained under him and dedicated themselves to the

maritime service, come to slap his back and ask if he
remembers them:

I tell you this is good; it tells you that once in your life you
had gone the right way to work. I have been thus slapped,
and I have winced, for the slap was heavy, and I have
glowed all day long and gone to bed feeling less lonely in
the world by virtue of that hearty thump. Don't I remember the little So-and-so's! I tell you I ought to know the
right kind of looks.

Yet immediately after his declaration of faith in the
ethical system of work—training young men to become
good seamen, and feeling he has contributed to a better
world by that work—Marlow expresses the fear Jim
excites in him. For Marlow says he would have trusted
the deck to Jim,

that youngster, on the strength of a single glance, and gone
to sleep with both eyes—and, by Jove, it wouldn't have
been safe. There are depths of horror in that thought. He
looked as genuine as a new sovereign, but there was some
infernal alloy in his metal. How much? The least thing—
the least drop of something rare and accursed; the least
drop!

The imagery that Conrad gives Marlow in this
speech provides enough clues to establish the motivation of Jim's fascination for Marlow. Marlow has always judged his trainees by "looks"—and hasn't he
always been right? Jim "looks" like them, looks like the
best specimen of them, and yet something beneath the
surface of Jim is different. That difference is what is so
frightening to Marlow, because it throws his own beliefs into doubt.

The experience is unsettling because in moving
into the interior underworld Marlow is leaving his bearings. He has been accustomed to rely on sense data—
physical fact, the look of things, the touch of a slap on

the back, the substance and achievement of work. Jim's spirit does not allow him this familiar route of experience.

Marlow expresses, though he may not be fully conscious of what he is saying, one of the levels of the abyss between illusion and reality. Through work—in the jungles of Patusan as a fighter and leader of men— Jim seems to find himself. In Patusan, Jim does not think about things; he acts. When he does "think"— that is, when he debates within himself an act of mercy and compassion to Gentleman Jim Brown rather than the self-interest of his own survival—he again causes disorder. Is then the reality of life to be found in carrying out established order? Is the striving for something better, even a gesture of presumed higher order, only equivalent to an illusion because such strivings are doomed to failure in the realistic world? Marlow does not fully explore these questions, because he knows that such introspection would impair his ability to function smoothly. He poses the questions nevertheless, keeping them at a safe distance, pushing them away when they threaten to seduce him. Marlow, a man who is moderate in everything, does not pass judgment on Jim. He concludes his tale in a haze, suggesting that the substance is still beyond him.

The French lieutenant who rescues the drifting *Patna* is, like Marlow, a man who allows himself little room for questions. A code of duty to which he adheres is all he needs. There are, however, three men who question and wonder about Jim's behavior. They are Captain Brierly, Gentleman Jim Brown, and Stein.

Captain Brierly, the officer who sat in judgment of Jim at the court of inquiry and wished Jim would "clear out," is before and throughout the inquiry akin to Marlow's unintellectual and unpretentious citizen. Shortly after Brierly finishes the inquiry and passes judgment, he commits suicide. Brierly is a minor character, but his suicide is an awesome event because it is an authorial comment on Jim's fatal idealism.

Brierly is one of those brave, courageous "stupid" people who cannot withstand the ugliness of truth. He has protected himself from doubt by a schedule of hard work and by adherence to an acknowledged system of law. Jim's case shatteres that routine. Brierly vaguely understands the threat Jim poses for him, and he tries to induce Jim to flee so that his trial cannot continue. Brierly goes so far as to attempt to bribe Jim. The painful absurdity is clear: the judge who tries to get the criminal to flee so that the judge will not have to pass sentence. Brierly's act represents a violation of the ethical and legal code. The fact that Jim refuses the offer does not alter the horrendous change that Brierly has undergone.

What is Brierly so afraid of? He has no crime of his own to hide. Yet Brierly says, "This infernal publicity is too shocking: there he [Jim] sits while all those confounded natives, serangs, lascars, quartermasters, are giving evidence that's enough to burn a man to ashes with shame. This is abominable. Why, Marlow, don't you think, don't you feel that this is abominable; don't you now—come—as a seaman? If he went away all this would stop at once."

Brierly's reaction suggests a cataclysmic fear of destruction of a total way of life. The fear is proved a short time later when Brierly "committed his reality and his sham together to the keeping of the sea." Marlow does not expatiate on the meaning of "sham"; he merely suggests Brierly's dilemma. Was Brierly living a life of sham? If he was, what was the sham? Was it the necessity of keeping a public image he knew to be false? It seems strange that a man would commit suicide because the reputation of his profession is being jeopardized.

In that last meeting he has with Marlow, Brierly

states his belief that the one thing which holds "us" together is "decency." This affair—Jim's affair— "destroys one's confidence." It is interesting to notice the choice of two words in Brierly's harangue. The first is "us." It echoes Marlow's reference to Jim as "one of us." Brierly is driven frantic by the shock of recognition that one of "us" would damage the fabric of a society in which he has been given a respectable part. Having remained wilfully blind to flaws in his society's code, Brierly cannot sustain the doubts Jim's case spreads.

The other word of importance in Brierly's tirade is "abominable," a word Brierly repeats in his hapless anger. Brierly's statement makes it apparent that Conrad, while not pursuing his fascination with abomination to the extent he did in *Heart of Darkness*, was very much concerned with it. In *Lord Jim*, Marlow is not yet ready to plunge into the abyss of abomination, but he is skirting its edges.

Conrad is fond of parallels. If Brierly recognizes in Jim a part of himself, the exposure of which drives Brierly to suicide, Jim recognizes reluctantly a part of himself in Gentleman Jim Brown. It is this recognition that leads Jim to his foolish, generous act of mercy to Brown and his gang. Instead of killing Brown—Jim and Dain Waris's warriors have effectively surrounded Brown and his gang—Jim offers Brown safe passage out of Patusan. Jim in his infinite romanticism believes Brown will be transformed by this act of mercy and charity.

What of Gentleman Jim Brown's attitude? Brown resents Jim's arrogance of grace: Lord Jim is not the Lord God able to forgive Brown his sins, as Brown will demonstrate to him. Brown does not take advantage of Jim when Jim comes unarmed to their truce conference, for he knows he "could do better than that"—he can destroy Jim's dream of a better world on Patusan in which he, Brown, has no part. Brown bides his time.

He waits until the dead of night to execute his massacre of the unsuspecting camp of Dain Waris, those fighters who have been lulled to sleep by Jim's belief that he has arranged peace on the island.

One final commentator remains to round out the observation of Jim. He is Stein, the wealthy merchant, the employer who sent Jim to Patusan. After hearing the story of Jim's death, Stein has "aged greatly." He is preparing to "leave all this"—his house, his possessions, and most important of all, the butterfly collection on which he has labored with love for many years. Stein's sadness can be attributed to his natural compassion for the young Jim, but the depths of that grief suggest a more complex state of feeling. For Stein, too, had become fascinated with Jim.

Stein believed he was a wise and experienced man who had been able to see the world as it really is, as well as how some men, like Jim, believed it should be. His attitude toward Jim was clearly paternal. He sent Jim to Patusan because the idealist needed a place in which he could hide from his shame. Having himself gone through many phases of life, Stein knew the chaos of youth, the pains of romanticism. The advice he gave Jim, "In the destructive element immerse," he had practiced himself. He had tasted the pleasures of nature in his butterfly-collecting expeditions, but he also knew how to compete on a more bloodthirsty level in his struggles for financial power. Both sides of Stein are epitomized in one episode: one morning on his way to catch butterflies in his net, he was accosted by three Malay pirates bent on killing him. Stein outwitted the pirates, killed them, and went forward with his butterfly expedition. Then he returned home to eat his normal breakfast.

Because of his nature, Stein had been drawn to the romantic Jim, and against his better judgment Stein had allowed himself to think of Jim as his natural heir. He

forgot that Jim could not immerse himself in the destructive element, the savage world of Gentleman Jim
Brown and the greedy world of the *Patna* and its captain and its owners. Stein's desire to have Jim bestride
the world of idealism and practicality as he, Stein, had
done, misled him into thinking Jim would come from
Patusan to take over Stein's realm.

With Jim's death Stein realizes he has no heirs: his
heritage will end with the passing of his own life. He
cannot even comfort Jim's mistress, Jewel, who, out of
grief at Jim's death and in flight from the violence
Brown has brought to Patusan, has come to live in his
house. Jewel is leading "a sort of soundless, inert life in
Stein's house." The last picture Marlow gives the reader
is that of the aged Stein waving his hand sadly at his
butterflies. He had wanted to will his collection, a
symbol of his way of life, to Jim. Perhaps he had
wanted to add Jim to his collection, in the way Marlow
had trained boys to become seamen. But Jim has es-
caped that net, choosing instead to "celebrate his piti-
less wedding with a shadowy ideal of conduct."

Conrad wrote out of the moral urgency of his
nature. His nervous energy and dramatic intensity often
seemed to have driven him to the breaking point. The
unforgettable intensity of some of his great scenes de-
rives from this sense of danger, of passion close to
bursting into disorder, of some meaning pregnant in
every utterance, in even the stillness of a place. These
scenes of sensual texture are also tantalizingly, insidi-
ously hued with larger symbolic and mysterious meaning. When Conrad succeeds on this level, he captures
the reader completely. Conrad's warning to the reader
about the seduction of ideas has its relevance here, for
Conrad's moral force and the reader's surrender to
Conrad's power of imagination result from the seduc-
tiveness of Conrad's ideas and speculations. *Lord Jim*

seduces the reader by its tantalizing, unending provocations of thought and idea.

With *Lord Jim* Conrad signaled his reliance on the idiosyncratic technique of shifts in points of view and in the chronology of narrative sequence. He also plunged further in his descent into the terrifying darkness of impulsive behavior, the journey into the underworld of psychic expression, and into the promise of a calm sea, a peace that integrates conscious and subconscious understanding at the end of the troubled, *necessary* journey. The journey in *Lord Jim* is *necessary* because of the psychological compulsions of its two major characters, Jim and Marlow. The necessity of undergoing the travails Jim experiences is a part of the mystery of Jim's character. It is as pointless to ask "why" Jim must shoulder his guilt to the grave and why he must indulge in excesses of romantic, sometimes adolescent and idealized concepts of behavior, as it is to ask "why" Hamlet cannot act out the intellectualized decisions he has made. Jim appeals to the reader because of his idealism, his excesses, his integrity. He is both foolish and magnificent. Ultimately, and maddeningly, it is impossible to forsake him, or to hold onto him.

3

The Dream-Nightmare:
Heart of Darkness

Heart of Darkness, which evolved from Conrad's experiences in his journey to Africa and along the Congo river in 1890, is foremost a literary achievement, but it is also a humanitarian and social document. Conrad knew he was writing on many levels, and in answer to the charge of vagueness and density, Conrad wrote to a friend, "I wish at first to put before you a general proposition: that a work of art is seldom limited to one elusive meaning and not necessarily tending to a definite conclusion. And for the reason that the nearer it approaches art, the more it acquires a symbolic character... the symbolic conception of a work of art has this advantage, that it makes a triple appeal covering the whole field of life. All the great creations of literature have been symbolic, and in that way have gained in complexity, in power, in depth and in beauty. I don't think you will quarrel with me on the ground of lack of precision; for as to precision of images and analysis my artistic conscience is at rest. I have given there all the truth that is in me; and all that the critics may say can make my honesty neither more nor less. But as to 'final effect' my conscience has nothing to do with that."

Heart of Darkness can be read then as a mystery story, a story of the mystery of character, with its intimations of fate. It can be read as an adventure story, the story of an African journey which the narrator,

Marlow, takes in his quest to meet the legendary Kurtz. The novella also reflects Conrad's anger at the barbarities of imperialistic greed. Above all, it is the record of a descent into the center of things, into the darkness at the core of existence.

Conrad's tale reverses the usual order of voyage from darkness to light, from hell upward to heaven as in the mythic world of Vergil and the Christian world of Dante. Marlow's journey in *Heart of Darkness* is made in several stages: he must pass through, both literally and spiritually, three stations known as the Outer, Central, and Inner Stations before he can see— and hear—the object of his search, Kurtz. The journey is one from a familiar world into an unfamiliar one, from a world which seems to hold the light of rational understanding to a world of instinctual darkness, a world which only can be grasped by a reason beyond the ordinarily reasonable.

The story of *Heart of Darkness* is told by Marlow who, as in *Lord Jim*, is a middle-aged man looking back on the experiences which have shaped him. Marlow begins his journey in Brussels, where he acquires, through an aunt's aid, a berth on a Belgian steamer which plies its trade on the Congo river. To reach his ship, which is anchored in Africa, he sets sail on a French steamer to Dakar. From there he makes his way to the Outer Station on the Congo. While on the journey to the Outer Station, he hears French cannon pouring into the African jungle. The bombardment seems to him unreal for there is no visible target; it seems an exercise in absurdity, a blow into a void. At the Outer Station Marlow is impressed again with a sense of absurdity when he views a boiler standing upside down in the jungle. He is shocked at his first view of African natives: starving, wasted figures, they are chained together and can hardly stand upright for lack of strength. He meets an accountant at the Station, who refers to

Kurtz as "a very remarkable man." The character of Kurtz begins to work on Marlow's imagination, but Marlow will have to wait many months before he can meet the "great" man. Marlow is forced, in fact, to wait ten days at the Outer Station before he can organize a caravan of sixty men to travel by foot the two hundred miles to the Central Station.

When Marlow reaches the Central Station fifteen days later, he finds the ship he has been appointed to command is at the bottom of the river. It had started out a few days earlier for the Outer Station to meet Marlow, but early in its voyage had been torn by river rocks and debris. Marlow manages to get the ship hauled ashore, but now is delayed in the repair of the ship for lack of rivets. For want of nails, he cannot go forward—the absurdity of such a small thing in the immensity of the jungle drives him to a manic display of dancing one night. Before Marlow gets his nails, he must spend many long days watching "pilgrims" arrive at and depart from the station. The "pilgrims" are traders, members of the Eldorado Expedition, in search of ivory, who travel by foot caravan for their booty. Marlow describes them sardonically: their faith is in the god of material wealth, they talk like sordid buccaneers. Marlow also becomes acquainted with the manager of the Station, and the manager's uncle. Both men speak of Kurtz, but in caustic tones. Because of their antagonism, Marlow is even more intrigued with discovering this mysterious man who can excite such opposite passions—respect and hatred—in various people.

Marlow finally sails on his ship to the Inner Station, with the manager on board. Before he reaches the Inner Station, his ship is attacked by natives loyal to Kurtz. The helmsman is pierced by an arrow, but the crew manage to disperse the attack and move into the Station. The first person Marlow meets there is the "harlequin," a Russian employee of the company, who is fiercely loyal to Kurtz. Marlow calls him the harlequin because the man is dressed in garish, motley costume. The harlequin declares that he, like Kurtz, can never return to "civilization"—he has seen too much in his association with Kurtz to go back to the conventions and veils of the European world. Then, at last, Marlow meets the mysterious Kurtz.

Marlow informs Kurtz that he has been sent to bring Kurtz back to Europe on the orders of the Belgian company which employs both of them. That night, Kurtz, though ill with fever, creeps out of his tent, and crawls along the ground to participate in a pagan ceremony outside his camp. It is the last rite in which Kurtz will participate, for he dies soon after being taken aboard Marlow's ship.

The experience at the Inner Station transforms Marlow utterly because the memory of Kurtz changes Marlow's view of the universe. When Marlow returns to England, he lies to Kurtz's fiancee, telling her that the "last word he pronounced was—your name." Marlow knows better, for he heard Kurtz's last words—"The horror! The horror!"—but he chooses not to dispel the illusion of the woman who wants to believe in Kurtz's greatness and self-sacrifice, who needs to believe in the illusion that Kurtz continued to try to bring light and morality to primitive and dark Africa.

Conrad's method in *Heart of Darkness* was to weave a tapestry of many complexities through his peculiar use of symbolic language. Symbols in Conrad are not given at one time fully; the reader gets the fullness of a Conradian symbol in stages, in voices heard and reheard with the phrase altered but the tone kept to the same pitch. In *Heart of Darkness* the word inscrutable is used repeatedly, in different circumstances, to describe both character and setting. Conrad is suggesting the difficulty of the mystery of character, perhaps of the meaning of the universe. Kurtz's African mistress, who is described as larger than life, a woman of immense stature, is also, in a key scene, called inscrutable. By this method of repetition, Conrad establishes a mood and consciousness deeper than the formally symbolic. The reference to "pilgrims" is another example of his method—the quest for greed (in pursuit of ivory) is thrown shockingly into association with Kurtz's earlier status as a missionary of technological progress, and with the dedication associated with zealots. The three stations Marlow must cross suggest the Christian Stations of the Cross, paths of pain and agony that must be traversed to reach a peace and understanding, and a fulfillment of one's appointed place on earth. Conrad's grim satire on this point is evidenced by the hyperbolic statements the manager of the Central Station makes, among them this one: "Each station should be like a beacon on the road towards better things, a centre for trade, of course, but also for humanising, improving, instructing."

An excellent example of the integrated functions of this interweaving may be seen in the use Conrad makes of clothing. On an obvious level, Marlow sees two women knitting in the anteroom of the Great Company in Brussels (which he describes as the "whited sepulchre city"). They are "guarding the door of Darkness," and "knitting black wool in a warm pall," because "not half, by a long way of those who shipped out to Africa ever came back to Europe." The company is responsible for many deaths through its mistreatment of African natives. Also, because of its ruthless drive for profits, the Company is willing to subject its employees to a brutalizing climate many of them cannot withstand.

The dress code, and lack of it, suggest another part of the meaning of the story. The Company accountant, who is always carefully groomed, is also inhuman when it comes to the groans of sick and dying men. Such noises "distract" the accountant from attention to his work. On the surface, the accountant seems a butt of Conrad's satire, for surely a man who values appearance above concern for humanity is not an object of admiration. Yet Conrad also suggests that the accountant keeps order. His way of dressing is a symbol of that order: he does not succumb to the "great demoralisation of the land."

To sustain order, then, seems to imply that certain cold, unfeeling, rigid lines of conduct must be observed. Otherwise one is led to the anarchy of dress—and of conduct—of the harlequin. Yet the harlequin, foolish as he is, is sympathetic to Marlow because of the unwavering loyalty the harlequin holds to Kurtz. At the end of the story, the harlequin is seen disappearing into the jungle to find a new habitation, because, like Kurtz, he has withdrawn from the civilized European world.

Conrad carefully places the accountant in the Outer Station, where things are seen from the outside, where order is imposed from without. The harlequin is, significantly, placed in the Inner Station, where order must come from within oneself, since all external authority, that of "civilization" anyway, has disappeared. Conrad convinces the reader that the harlequin must forsake his place in Western society if he is to continue, honestly, his unconventional life. Conversely, the accountant will never experience the depth of passion known by Kurtz, the harlequin, and their like.

The accountant's range of experience is also more restricted and narrow than that of Marlow, who has at least "peeped over the edge" in his meeting with Kurtz. The accountant does his job, and for him his way of life is rewarding: he is not aware of what he may be missing. But, then, he has never gone beyond the Outer Station.

Images of light and darkness also provide their

shade of meaning to the story. There is plenty of "light"
at the Outer Station, but it is a light that does not
penetrate into the center of things. At the Inner Station,
the heart of darkness, Marlow finds a glimmer of
understanding. Sound and silence also accompany the
journey:

Going up that river was like traveling back to the earliest
beginnings of the world, when vegetation rioted on the
earth and the big trees were kings. An empty stream, a great
silence, and an impenetrable forest. . . . It was the stillness
of an implacable force brooding over an inscrutable intention.

The mystery of Kurtz's personality is finally
glimpsed through Conrad's interweaving of layers of
meaning. It is profoundly important for Marlow to
understand Kurtz because "all Europe made Kurtz."
Kurtz then is a significant representative of Western
character. He was always a man of excess: in his youth,
a fervent, passionate zealot for Western, technological
progress; at the end of his life, a captive of primitive
rites who decorated his house with totem poles adorned
with human heads. Yet, in spite of Kurtz's excesses, or
rather because of them, Marlow is drawn to him. Kurtz,
Marlow affirms, was a "remarkable man. He had something to say. He said it."

Kurtz fascinates Marlow because Kurtz is different
from other men. He has stepped beyond the bounds of
moderation, having crossed the dividing line between
humanity and the pursuit of the dream of strange
knowledge. While Kurtz "had stepped over the edge,"
Marlow "had been permitted to draw back by hesitat-
ing feet." Hesitation—Marlow's sense of his limitations—saved Marlow from "that inappreciable moment
of time in which we step over the threshold of the in-
visible." But Marlow has not been entirely spared: the
knowledge he has gained no longer permits him to har-

bor a sunny world of illusion. For the rest of his life he will bear the picture of the darker side of man. Perhaps Marlow's greatest moment comes at the end of the story, when knowing the truth, he does not state it to Kurtz's fiancee. He chooses to allow her to continue to live in a world of sunny illusion, a world from which he has now been cast out.

The Marlow of *Heart of Darkness*, though he is younger and less experienced, is very much like the Marlow of *Lord Jim*. In both stories, he is the decent man, one committed to moderation and common sense, yet obsessed in his attempt to fathom the passions of magnificently flawed fellow creatures. Lord Jim and Kurtz, though one can be seen as fallen angel and the other as devil, are as alike in Conrad's scheme as they are different in their means of gratification. Marlow said of Kurtz, "Whatever he was, he was not common." The nameless narrator of *Lord Jim* said of Jim he was a man of exquisite, not common, sensibility. Both Kurtz and Lord Jim were impossible visionaries who could not halt the progress of their vision, nor turn their backs on the paths into which their dreams led them. Both were outside the ordinary ken, both died in the cause of their egoistic pursuit of knowledge and sensation, and yet both had the potential of great talents and gifts to convey to other men. The extraordinary power of *Heart of Darkness*, as of *Lord Jim*, stems from the urgency with which Conrad expresses the fascination of the dream and the timeless mystery of character.

For example, at the beginning of *Heart of Darkness*, Marlow compares the dark Thames, where he is telling his story, to the dark Congo. He alludes to the conquest of Britain by the Roman Empire, and to the philosophical defense of that imperial conquest. (Conrad had written a passage in the manuscript, which he excised from the printed version, that made obvious a comparison between the Roman conquest and the

Western exploitation of Africa. The point of the comparison was to belittle the high-sounding claims of European imperialists in their plunder of Africa.) Conrad's attack on imperialism was both specific and moral. In particular he abhorred the barbaric treatment by European conquerers of African natives, the destruction of ancient civilizations by arrogant men bringing not light but destruction, not progress but moral decline. In a more philosophical and less historic perspective, he was condemning force without reason (or right reason, if the reader prefers). Conrad knew that imperialists, men in power, could always manufacture rationalizations for their actions through their ownership of communications media and through foundations and Societies for the Propagation of Any Things. Yet if Conrad condemned force without reasonable morality, he also decried reason without a corresponding morality. For Conrad, intellectual analysis, theorizing, and philosophic rationalizations without concern for the common feelings and emotional, cultural attitudes of people were as monstrous as physical mistreatment and brutality.

In his portrait of Kurtz, Conrad exhibits both aspects of this unbalanced arrogance. Kurtz had gone to Africa with a missionary-like goal: he was going to bring "light" to a "dark" continent. As trader, as imperialist, as ivory-hunter, the material rewards of his commerce would bring progress to a "primitive" race. Once at his ivory trading station, Kurtz succumbed to total indulgence in sensation. He forgot his propaganda, but he also abandoned his proportion, his sense of human limits. What started then as a dream for Kurtz ended as nightmare, and for Kurtz there was no end to the nightmare except in his death. Marlow expresses his empathetic agony of Kurtz's experience when he says, "I remained to dream the nightmare out to the end."

4

The Sea Stories

Conrad's fondness for "journeys" as a literary means by which to convey a change or development in character is evidenced most strongly in his sea stories. In these stories the distance between innocence and maturity, ignorance and awareness is spanned by a "test" which the hero, usually a young officer, undergoes at sea. Though Conrad's sea stories are seemingly simple tales, they are as much metaphor and symbol as his longer work.

It is easy to speculate that in the sea stories Conrad is reliving those moments when he was young, when the world was fresh and promise was still an operative word. Indeed, the plot details and use of settings, as well as repeated returns to people he had known for his models, show that Conrad was literally forging his way into fiction from his "background." But there is more to it than that, for Conrad also uses his "background" in his novels.

Because of the nature of the short story, Conrad speaks even more symbolically than he does in the novel. It is an important fact to keep in mind, because the short story is limited in space; its effects must be given in compressed form, and consequently it is often more intense, the language more telescoped than the longer work. Conrad's shorter work may then be said to be intensely symbolic. The language speaks on two levels concurrently.

What Conrad really sought in his "sea stories" was the command of experience. The fact that so many of these sea stories are concerned with the first command of the young hero, the step that divides a leader from his men on a personal level as well as joins him with them in a solidarity of enterprise, is evidence of Conrad's abiding interest in the nature of personal discipline and public responsibility. The distinctive touch in Conrad's five major sea stories is a storm—a physical crisis by which character is tested and molded. Conrad varied the details, most of which came from his days as a seaman, but the structure and perspective of events reflect one central vision.

While the "sea stories" are metaphoric journeys, they are, as well, direct and easily comprehensible events of narrative action. Conrad never lost his fondness for the works of Frederick Marryat and James Fenimore Cooper, writers he read in his youth and who provided models for clear narrative action. Conrad always kept in mind the simple heroism that was the territory of the young to seize. He understood the charm of action for the young, the need to throw oneself into experience with enthusiasm. Had he not done it all himself in the south of France, and later, in a more chastened mood, in the British maritime service?

"Youth," which Conrad published as the title story in a collection in 1902 (the other two were *Heart of Darkness* and "The End of the Tether") was one of Conrad's favorite works. He dubbed it a "feat of memory." An easy task of writing, the story was finished in a few days in late May and June of 1898. Conrad's source for the story was his experience as second mate on board the *Palestine* from September 1881 to April 1883.

"Youth" begins with a sentence placing the story: "This could have occurred nowhere but in England." Throughout the story Marlow will refer to his experience as an English one. When he describes the crew's efforts during a storm, he identifies the strength and spirit of the men as English.

The story Marlow tells is simple: the first voyage to the East and the first voyage as second mate of the young, eager Marlow. The trip also marks the first command of the ship's young captain. Thus the story is about both the time of youth and the freshness of experience as seen through older eyes. Youth and innocence at their most appealing set sail. Experience will test them with a storm at sea. The *Judea*, which had been put in mothballs when its owner went bankrupt, is covered with rust, grime, and soot, but to Marlow's young eyes it is an image of beauty.

The spirit of the seamen and their captain surmount the number of small mishaps that bedevil the ship. When fire breaks out and an explosion rips the cargo deck, the crew and the captain do not consider any change in their destination: they will fulfill their bargain, arrive at their appointed destination.

Even as the fire is roaring, the captain orders the crew to trim the yards of the deck. Following his command, men in rags, their faces covered with coal dust and ash, mop up the deck to make it shipshape. As Marlow says, remembering the absurd, magnificent, disarming scene: "O youth! the strength of it, the faith of it, the imagination of it."

The *Somerville*, a steamer that catches sight of the *Judea*, attempts to tow the burning ship into port. When the fire on the *Judea* threatens to spread to the *Somerville*, the men on the *Judea* cut the towline. They hope still to make it to port, to salvage their ship, which has become a part of them, as they of it. Finally, they acquiesce to the reality of the situation, abandon the burning hulk, and jump into lifeboats.

Marlow punctuates his tale, which he is telling to his cronies, with an injunction to "pass the bottle." A bottle of claret rests on a table around which the five old seamen have gathered. Marlow is nowhere else in Conrad's work as genial as he is here. His libations, his humor in describing his own "command" (he is in charge of one of the lifeboats), his encounter with a blaspheming skipper when he reaches shore, are all the stuff of nourishing comedy. For Marlow is saying, what harm can the illusions of youth cause? Indeed, look at how much they accomplish—they provide a focus for the anarchic, struggling forces in young men.

"Youth" is one of Conrad's most appealing and most sentimental stories. In other tales he will expose the dangers of sentimentality, the pitfalls of insularism and prejudice. Here he is content, like an old man mellowed and ripened, to enjoy the fellowship and sensual pleasure that the recollection of his youthful illusions bring.

"Typhoon," which Conrad published in a second short-story collection in 1902, is the story of an older seaman at the height of his powers. It differs from "Youth" in that the sentimental notion of all men rising to the occasion is no longer in evidence: some men meet the crisis well, others poorly; all are exposed by it. Although "Typhoon" is told in the third-person authorial voice, its viewpoint is that of the type of man Marlow represents.

Captain MacWhirr, the hero of "Typhoon," is introduced as a dull, unglamorous figure. He is endowed with many of the qualities of Marlow—a belief in the virtue of work, an idealization of common sense and physical discipline, and a distrust of intellectuality. He has given up the romantic notions he held in his youth: he is a practical, down-to-earth leader of men who need discipline. His "mind" is described as possessing such qualities as "firmness and stupidity." MacWhirr owns enough imagination to get him through each successive day; for him that is enough. He distrusts imagination because it leads to speculation and questioning. Yet Conrad is confessing his admiration for this seemingly dull man who knows how to keep order when he is threatened by various kinds of storm. Perhaps there is a personal reason for Conrad's affection: MacWhirr bears some resemblance to his creator in their love of adventure and the sea. MacWhirr ran off to sea when he was fifteen, leaving his Belfast grocer father astounded. This flight parallels Conrad's decision when he was seventeen to leave his homeland for France, and the sea.

MacWhirr's common sense comes to the fore in an early incident. The *Nan-Shan* has been transferred from a European registry to a Siamese flag. The junior officer Jukes finds it difficult to work under a Siamese flag. MacWhirr cannot understand Jukes's discomfort. So long as the flag is hung properly, he does not see what the matter is.

Two crises occur, and in both of them MacWhirr keeps his head while his subordinate officers go to pieces. Since it is MacWhirr's decision to meet the storm, he must overcome it. The story is a record of that test, of MacWhirr's spirit in the face of the storm he has refused to evade. At one point, pushed about by debris and the swirling waters, Jukes is thrown into the arms of MacWhirr, to whom he clings. The picture is graphic: a young, intellectually-trained officer submitting to the experienced older man.

MacWhirr shows his sense of order in another way. The storm tosses about the possessions of the Chinese passengers, and their hoard of silver pieces scatters over the deck. In the midst of the storm, MacWhirr orders Jukes to collect the pieces, for he will not have any fighting over money on his ship.

Finally the storm abates. Before leaving his ship, which he has now brought to port, MacWhirr parcels out the silver pieces that Jukes and the crew had gathered. Preserving his notion of law and justice—though some may argue that he assumes an arbitrary power here—MacWhirr divides the silver pieces equally among the Chinese passengers.

"Typhoon" glorifies the simple man uninfected by ideas. For some men a "stupid" blind faith in the right virtue is enough to enable them to get through life well. To upset such men with foreign ideas—all ideas except the few simple ones of honor and duty—is contrary to the law of their human nature. Other men are not so fortunate however. They are born with imagination, and their imagination will lead them to tragedy or chastening experience.

In "The End of the Tether" Conrad draws a portrait of another simple seaman. He possesses courage and steadfastness, a "stupid and firm" grasp on what he considers the verities. Whalley, after a competent career as ship's officer distinguished by faith in the maritime code and by good work, retires. He had planned to leave his savings to his only child, his daughter who now lives in impoverished circumstances in Australia (Whalley's wife had died some time ago). Circumstances however provide a rude shock for him: the bank in which he had deposited his money fails. With his last 500 pounds, Whalley buys a half-interest in an old ship, the *Sofala*, owned by Massy, a man consumed with one desire: to win the Manilla lottery and retire to live off the fat of the land.

Whalley's investment is partly a loan. He is to be paid back his 500 pounds at the end of three years, provided that he serve as captain of the *Sofala* for that length of time. If he should leave before he has served three years, Massy can delay payment of the loan. The captain is at the end of his tether because he discovers in the second year that he is going blind. To admit to his blindness, to give up his captaincy, would mean the possible loss of his 500 pounds. Whalley is obsessed with leaving this pitiable fortune to his daughter. In pursuit of the obsession, he commits an act contrary to all his tenets of maritime honor. He hides the fact of his near-blindness, he endangers the safety of the ship and its crew.

Because of his trusted servant, a Serang, who does his bidding without asking any questions, Whalley is able to hide his growing blindness. The Serang is his pilot, but the pilot is blind to his master's blindness Massy also remains blind to it because of his own obsession with self-pity and greed. One crew member, Sterne, the mate who holds a bitter hatred for all his superiors, all the people in the world he believes have deceived and exploited him, discovers the secret. Sterne believes he has found the opportunity, finally, to get command of a ship; he will use his knowledge to blackmail Whalley.

Circumstances however upset Sterne's scheme. In a fit of greed, Massy decides to sink his ship for the insurance money. Placing iron bars near the compass point to deflect the ship's course, Massy watches as Whalley, blind to the ruse, feels the ship strike the reefs.

Massy's final confrontation with Whalley drives home several points. In Whalley's cry, "You shall pay for this," is the echo of the money Massy owes Whalley, the debt he will never pay. In Massy's cry, "You blind devil! It's you that drove me to it," is the accusation hurled with some justification at the blind man. Whalley is blind in several ways: he will not accept the fact of his impotence, the fact that he cannot give a financial legacy to his only child (who has a husband and a home, no matter how poor both of them may be, in Australia). Whalley retains a steely reserve in the face of Massy's vulgar pleas for some kind of limited fellowship; in this sense, he exhibits an emotional as well as intellectual disdain for the unpleasant, the undisciplined, the seamy underside of life. Perversely, Whalley's silence in response to Massy's taunts about his wealth result in Massy's belief that Whalley is engaging in deception, that Whalley has more money than he admits to. Having made up his mind that Whalley is wealthy and will not help him with a new loan to repair the ship, Massy explodes in a fit of hatred for Whalley. His decision to sink the ship for the insurance money—his final desperate act for money—comes after he has made his mistaken assumptions about Whalley. Conrad, in his uncanny ability to suggest guilt on all sides, implies Whalley may be "guilty" in refusing to reach out to Massy, to communicate with a more unfortunate being.

The two men represent a philosophical contrast as well as forces in a psychological confrontation. On one side is an older order, symbolized by Whalley and his sailing ship, *The Condor*, now at the bottom of the sea. On the other side is ranged a modern world, fittingly represented by men of greed and petty ambition, Massy and Sterne, and by their ship, the *Sofala*, a steamer whose boilers constantly break down and spew ugly ash. Whalley, who has a chance to leave the *Sofala* before she sinks, does not take the opportunity. Choosing to go down with his ship, he loads his pockets with the iron bars Massy had used to deflect the ship's course. He ends his life in a world he cannot abide by utilizing the tools of that newer world—the iron bars—as the means by which to escape from that world.

After the climax, Conrad supplies a few concluding details. Mr. Van Wyck, the wealthy tobacco planter who had guessed Whalley's blindness and who had befriended the old man by keeping the secret, is so distressed over the news of Whalley's death that he leaves the Orient to return to Holland and retirement. Van Wyck realizes that he and his values have become irrelevant in the modern world.

Whalley's last letter to his daughter is also presented, as well as the scene of the daughter reading the letter. The enormous love Whalley bore for his daughter impresses itself on the woman far away in a boarding house in Australia. She feels remorse at the lost opportunity to have shown him a greater affection. The final scene is necessary, thematically, for this reason: the world which the daughter inhabits is drab and colorless. Whalley had wanted better things for her, but just as he could not stop time's destruction of his powers, he cannot stop the new times from dealing harshly with her. Whalley in the end leaves nothing to his daughter, for she does not even inherit the truth of the story of his last command. Though it would have been a bitter legacy, it would at least have been an offering.

Critics have commented on the reserve of style in "The End of the Tether." A diffuse story, it contains a series of small effects lacking in the intensity of a single dominating action. Its hero is not a tragic figure, someone defeated by the questing magnificence of his illusions. Rather, he is a decent man whom circumstances have warped pitiably. Even in Whalley's last moments, Conrad offers him only sympathy, not an embrace of the heart: for the captain's last moments have a discordant note about them—Whalley and Massy screaming at each other, hurling petty accusations at each other amidst the roar of the storm-tossed waves.

After "The End of the Tether" Conrad began the writing of *Nostromo* and the series of sketches that became *The Mirror of the Sea*. In both these works the sailor-heroes are men of bravado and eccentricity. The humility of Whalley, the doubts and hesitancy of Marlow, the modesty of MacWhirr give way to the splendor of Nostromo and the hard, gritty, colorful brilliance of Dominic Cervoni. Cervoni, who appears in five of Conrad's books, twice under his own name (in *The Mirror of the Sea* and *The Arrow of Gold*) is the seaman *par excellence.* Cervoni is Conrad's impossible ideal, his reverse Don Quixote, the brigand knight. It is an ideal intensified because of the inalterable fact that Conrad could not will away his own intellect and intellectual tolerance and indecision; he could only admire the primitive Cervoni whose purity (in less idealized figures it might be called narrowness or stubbornness of spirit) is impregnable to modernity and modish ideas.

In his attitude to Dominic Cervoni, Conrad exhibits the appeal that physical strength allied with firmness of decision and freedom of action have for him. Cervoni is able to make order out of chaos, particularly in a storm when things fall asunder, slide away from their appointed place in the universe of the ship, when for an agony of psychological time it seems as if the world has come apart. Cervoni has enough ego—the gift of his primitive instinct for survival, the sense of his own mastery of nature and of men—to conquer the storms and put his ship back in order. In several of Conrad's tales, it is the primitive, unlettered (and therefore in some ways Conrad seems to be saying, unfettered) male who conquers the terror of the unknown. None of these men match, however, the loving particularity Conrad shows for Cervoni. It is Conrad's educated man—the sensitive young captain—who falters, who must paradoxically learn anew to be "natural" with his men, to know the unwritten rules which harness energy at the same time they release it. Like a law of physics, Conrad's ideal heroes are balanced in nature, physically attuned to it, able to ride the storm through to the calm. His failed heroes—magnificent, troubled, intellectual, incomplete in some way—cannot balance their physical and spiritual natures. They are overcome by paralysis. Even if the immediate cause of their deaths is an intrusion by worldly evil into an idyllic world created out of clean, fresh pristine nature, as in the second halves of *Lord Jim* and *Victory*, the sense of inevitability that the dream must be shattered, that personal retreat into an idyllic setting is only a temporary and precarious balance in the tightrope of life, pervades the tale.

Two of these young sensitive heroes who face a test of command at sea, and who may be said to be in direct relationship to Cervoni literarily as Conrad was to Cervoni personally, are the subjects of two later sea stories, "The Secret Sharer" and "The Shadow-Line." Probably the best-known and most anthologized of all of Conrad's work, "The Secret Sharer" exists on at least two levels: the ship's real sea journey and the young captain's psychic one. On the simplest level it is an adventure: a young officer who has accidentally killed one of his crew swims one night to the *Sephora*, anchored nearby. The young captain of the *Sephora* is walking the deck alone. He sees the dripping figure rise from the sea like a "headless corpse," and spread his shadow over the precincts of the ship; the sense persists that the young captain, having sent all his men below deck earlier that night, has been preparing for this visit, has been waiting for it.

The young captain hears the story of the circumstances that drove his visitor, Leggatt, to the deck. The "headless corpse"—the captain's double, his secret sharer—tells him that during the melee of a storm he struck one of the sailors who was slack in his duty. In falling, the seaman hit his head on the deck and died immediately. The young officer, Leggatt, was confined to quarters under suspicion of manslaughter, but he managed to escape and swim to the *Sephora*. His great and poignant fear is that of being locked away from the open sea and air. All his life he had trained for the calling of seaman, and now that life, in one moment and as a result of a thoughtless, impulsive act, is over for him.

The double's first name is given only once. The

captain says, "It was Archbold—but at this distance of years I hardly am sure." Yet the captain never addresses the stranger by his first name, for to do so would distinguish him as an individual. Conrad's purpose is to create "Archbold" as part of the captain's psyche. The reader is left to ponder the reality of the young officer: did he exist, or was he an image dredged out of the captain's subconscious in order to recognize and accept his potentiality for disorder?

The captain, who must decide on whether to shelter the fugitive or surrender him to the authorities, does not inform on the criminal who comes to his abode for shelter. At considerable risk to himself, he feeds, clothes, and hides him in his cabin. He puts him in a "sleeping suit," a phrase that, particularly in the context of this story, suggests the unconscious.

The captain finally sets his double free by having him jump ship and swim to a nearby shore ("a free man, a proud swimmer striking out for a new destiny"). But in helping Leggatt to a new life, the captain must take the ship dangerously close to the reefs. In turn, it is the fugitive's hat which the captain had given to him to shield him from the sun that protects the captain and his ship. The white hat, falling from the swimmer's head (he had first come to the ship as a "headless corpse"), floats on the water and serves as the buoymarker by which the captain safely navigates the ship away from the reefs.

The voyage to the other side of his self has thus made the young captain whole.

Many critics have seen in "The Secret Sharer" Conrad's clearest statement of the concept of freedom as integration of the divided parts of one's self. In order to achieve unity of self, the individual must accept his potentiality for evil, and realize that fugitive and captain, criminal and policeman, may be created by circumstance or by character. Conrad was however not so naive as to urge law-abiding citizens to lay down their vigilance in a saintly, mindless embrace of the criminal. He had once written to his friend, R. B. Cunninghame-Grahame: "Fraternity means nothing unless the Cain-Abel business." Conrad was aware of the criminal impulse, but he also knew there was a way to integrate, if not eradicate, the perversities of human nature through an acceptance of the opposite, complementary drives that are indivisible parts of human nature.

Conrad wrote "The Secret Sharer" in November 1909 but did not publish it until 1913 in the volume *'Twixt Land and Sea.* He was having difficulties with the writing of his novel *Chance*, and he turned to other works for re-invigoration. In 1909 he finished *A Personal Record* and *Under Western Eyes* in the same flow of energy that carried him through "The Secret Sharer." In all three works Conrad is exploring the divisions of the self, and the attempts one can make at attaining a wholeness of spirit. In "The Secret Sharer," the mood, the tone, the resolution of the narrative all can be characterized as a chasteness of telling that makes it apparent Conrad had found a way to express an innate harmony which in his earlier work he only achieved fitfully. Metaphorically, he has come home, to himself. In Douglas Hewitt's words, the story is an "allegory of Conrad's future development."

Conrad's last major sea story was "The Shadow-Line." Because he drew upon the memory of his first command aboard the *Otago* in 1888, he called the story "exact autobiography." Conrad wrote the story for his son Borys, who at the time was fighting in the trenches of World War I. The story reflects Conrad's desire to show his son, and his young readers, that war and battle and crisis are not new, that even the present holocaust could be surmounted as the wars in Conrad's time and his father's times were. The story also reveals Conrad's sense of divided loyalties—for World War I made him more conscious of the conflicts of his allegiance. He was a naturalized British citizen of Polish origin; his son was fighting in France; the Russians were allies of the British and French. If the Western allies won the war, then the Russian empire and its subjugation of Poland would continue.

In "The Shadow-Line" a young captain newly appointed to his command must rid his ship of its "ghosts"—that is, its associations with past failures. One of the "ghosts" is the memory of the late captain, who had viciously prayed for the ship to go down with him as he lay dying, and who threw his fiddle overboard so that no one would have the pleasure of it after his death. Another of the "ghosts" is Burns, the chief mate under the mad captain. When Burns falls ill, the new young captain has his chance to be rid of him. But the young captain knows that to leave Burns on shore in a hospital would be an evasion of responsibility, that of meeting and dealing with men unlike himself and establishing a bond between them. He has Burns brought back to the ship from the hospital. As the journey continues, and a storm arises, Burns grows worse, he raves like the dead, mad captain, and in his wraithlike figure Burns becomes a reflection of the phantasmal journey the ship is taking.

In spite of many obstacles, the captain succeeds in his "test." He and his crew survive the loss of the quinine which had been thrown overboard by the mad captain in a fit of hatred for mankind, hatred because everyone else on the ship was alive while he was dying. Helping the young captain in his trials is Ransome, the cook, a sailor afflicted with a weak heart. Ransome gives heart to the men by his example of tireless work and undaunted devotion to the captain and the ship. It is perhaps obvious symbolism here—the physical weak-in-heart keeps his morale, never surrenders to apathy, depression, or exhaustion. Yet the intensity of Conrad's vision, his seemingly cool gaze on passions that excite him, are irresistible in their appeal to the reader.

Miraculously the ship weathers its storm. Burns reappears on deck, having passed the crisis of his madness. The ship heads to port, with all men safe.

"The Shadow-Line" is a lyric prose poem. It idealizes the experience of the "test" of the young hero. In his recounting of the captain's journey, Conrad dedicates the story to the ship's crew, "worthy of my undying regard."

Conrad's sea stories, in which the ship is at the center of the universe, are among his most popular work. They tend at times to suffer from a sentimentality born of idealization of the hard work-success ethic. Yet the love Conrad bore the sea, and his admiration of those men who tested their physical skills and moral codes against its demands, surmount all petty criticism. Conrad's sea stories, like his other work, are visions of the dream that, in T. S. Eliot's words, "passeth understanding." The difference is that, in the sea stories, the dreams are possible of attainment. Or, as Conrad wrote in *Chance*:

I have observed that profane men living in ships, like the holy men gathered together in monasteries, develop traits of profound resemblance. This must be because the service of the sea and the service of a temple are both detached from the vanities and errors of a world which follows no severe rule. The men of the sea understand each other very well in their view of earthly things, for simplicity is a good counsellor and isolation not a bad educator. A turn of mind composed of innocence and scepticism is common to them all, with the addition of an unexpected insight into the motives, as of disinterested lookers-on at a game.

5

Politics in Action:
Nostromo

Conrad's definition of politics is morality in action. Given such a wide-ranging and broad definition, politics is everywhere in Conrad's work. Even the most apolitical and amoral man is involved in politics as long as he exists on a planet populated by other creatures. In Conrad's fiction his protagonists are constantly trying to resolve the conflict in themselves between the desire for isolation and for community. They come to terms with their isolation by an acceptance, limited as it may be, of their communal, or political, responsibilities. Despair, for example, drives Almayer (in *Almayer's Folly*) and Heyst (in *Victory*) to burn their houses, after their one remaining tie to a wider community—Almayer's love for his daughter Nina, Heyst's love for Lena—is taken from them.

In *Nostromo*, which Conrad published in 1904, he is more overtly political than in his earlier fiction. *Nostromo* is a portrait of politics in a Central American state, but it is, more profoundly, a study of various individuals testing their faiths against opposition and revealing, through their actions, their morality.

The presentation of the order of events in *Nostromo* is highly intricate. In the first 120 pages the chronology and point of view shift at least five times. Conrad justified the use of his technique by the claim that he was working to achieve the illusion of immediacy of consciousness in the reader. Though the action of the novel takes place over a period of time, the sense of time is always the present; awareness of events crowds in on the reader, as an incident in the present reminds him of past occurrences, and an occurrence in the past conveys present tensions. Nevertheless, the canvas of characters, setting and time of *Nostromo* is so diverse that the cries of dismay of those first viewing it are understandable. There are however several lines that, if held fast to, will enable the reader to get a perspective of the material.

The first line to draw is the narrative sequence of events, not as Conrad gives them, but as they can be reconstructed by the reader:

Like a magic mountain, the "silver of the mine" stands above the Occidental Province of the Republic of Costaguana. The San Tome mine is managed by Charles Gould, who inherited it from his father. Saddled with debts, the San Tome mining company had suspended operations, but it is rescued by Gould through the financial aid of the American millionaire Holroyd. Holroyd is pictured as a missionary who believes that "material interest"—industrialization and technocracy—inevitably brings prosperity and progress to primitive countries. If Holroyd is a missionary, Gould is an idealist. For him the mine has become child, lover, and mistress.

Ribiera, a progressive politician, has gained power as the result of the general well-being of the country; the country's economic state of health, in turn, is based on the workings of the silver mine. Now, Ribiera's general, Montero, corrupted by his vanity into believing himself the people's savior (as many have called him), revolts against Ribiera and attempts to set up his own government. The revolt spreads from the capital city in the interior of the country to the outlying provinces, one of which is the Occidental Province.

In Sulaco, the capital city of the Occidental Province, the Goulds, Martin Decoud, Father Corbellan, Antonia Avellanos, Don Jose Avellanos, Dr. Monygham, and others wait for news of Ribiera's effort to suppress Montero's revolt. Charles Gould assumes a neutrality in the battle, for he acts only for and in his mine—Costaguana, indeed the world, is of little interest to him.

Martin Decoud, the Costaguanan, a man of keen intelligence and coruscating wit, represents one view in Nostromo: that of the skeptical philosopher who sees human folly as a permanent condition of mankind. Decoud, who loves Antonia Avellanos, works with the liberals in Sulaco for a more enlightened rule. His intelligence constantly reminds him of the futility of trying to improve the conditions of the human race. Nevertheless, Decoud's love for Antonia, and his regard for her wishes, lead him into the political activity for which he holds no hope, and thus no enthusiasm, but in which Antonia believes wholeheartedly.

Brilliant and cynical, Decoud sees one way out of the folly of the recurrent revolutions in Costaguana—they are folly for Decoud because revolutions, for him, signal only a change in command. Decoud puts forth the idea of the separation of the Occidental Province from the rest of Costaguana. He convinces his circle of friends that the plan is viable: the Occidental Province needs nothing from the Republic.

The forces of the invading army move closer to Sulaco, and Nostromo, a brave, valiant, fighting man is asked to help save a hoard of silver that has been transported from the mine to Sulaco. The enlightened men and women of the Occidental Province reason with Nostromo that only he can save the silver—and thus the Province—since he is the best seaman in the country. Only he can get a ship loaded with a cargo of silver to a hiding place on a deserted island off the coast of Sulaco. Nostromo's interest, up to this point, has been in the self-fulfillment that comes with a day's work well done. He is not concerned with the workings, or even the rewards, of politics. At the last moment before the ship sails, Martin Decoud goes on board, planning to remain with the silver on the island. Unknown to them, Hirsch, a merchant, has also slipped on board.

A ship commanded by a Montero ally, Sotillo, steaming from the north to invade the Occidental Province, collides with Nostromo's ship in the dark of night. Nostromo's ship survives the collision and limps to its appointed destination. Here the silver is hidden. Nostromo leaves Decoud and returns to Sulaco in order to be aware of the developing situation. Decoud remains on the island, because as propagandist for the Occidental "Republic" and as foe of Montero he is a wanted man. Left alone, Decoud is unable to bear the isolation. His sense of futility is so great, and his need for some human voice to dissuade him from futility so intense, that he commits suicide.

In Sulaco, the merchant Hirsch, who had been swept aboard the enemy ship commanded by Sotillo in the impact of the collision, is tortured by Sotillo, who wants to know the location of the missing silver. Hirsch mumbles the astounding truth about Nostromo's one-man sea-lift, but Sotillo in his hysteria refuses to believe him.

Dr. Monygham, who, like Decoud, has a skeptic's view of human nature (but who is redeemed to humanity through his idealized love of Mrs. Gould), meets Nostromo after Nostromo has returned to Sulaco. Their meeting place is in the empty building near the harbor, where the dead body of Hirsch, shot by Sotillo in rage, hangs. Monygham assumes Nostromo's ship has been sunk, and the treasure lost. (He, along with the Goulds,

Martin Decoud, Antonia, her brother Don Jose Avellanos, had put their faith in this marvelous "capataz de
cargadore.")

Nostromo does not disabuse Monygham of his
assumption, and it is in the moral abuse by omission
that Nostromo's corruption begins. The silver tongue of
the mine has begun its invidious communication with
the man who up to now has been deaf to the chants of
material temptation. Monygham, realizing he must gain
time for the loyal forces of the Occidental "Republic,"
creates a plan whereby he deceives Sotillo into believing
that Hirsch was indeed lying and that the silver lies
buried in the waters beneath the harbor.

While Sotillo dredges the harbor, Monygham in-
structs Nostromo to run a train from Sulaco through
enemy lines in order to deliver new battle plans to
Sulaco's loyal General Barrios. Barrios has become the
head of military operations for Occidental indepen-
dence. Again, Nostromo comes to the rescue. The serio-
comic image of the iron monster, with the brightly clad
Nostromo atop it, chugging in a cloud of steam through
the mountains and lush countryside is one of the high
points in the novel. Nostromo succeeds in his mission,
and Barrios and his aide, the bandit-turned-soldier
Hernandez, defeat the Montero forces. Sulaco and the
Occidental "Republic" are saved from the invading
armies.

Asked a price for his aid, Nostromo replies that
honor is enough compensation. Later he will feel
cheated, "used" by the victorious forces. Nostromo,
who has no political beliefs and who has shunned political activity heretofore, feels the measure of a man lies
in individual acts of heroism, in meeting daily chal-
lenges with ingenuity. This faith in personal fulfillment,
in the belief that the universe will be well off as long as
individuals find self-satisfaction in their work, weakens
when he returns to the deserted island and finds no

trace of Decoud. Instinctively he knows Decoud is dead. (Decoud had rowed out to sea and shot himself under a blazing sun.) Nostromo, believing in the ethic of loyalty and comradeship until the job is done, feels Decoud has betrayed him, and, by that betrayal, is mocking all Nostromo represents. Other reasons—all connected with this sense Nostromo develops of having been "used," taken from his natural element and pushed into a world he does not comprehend—are suggested; the disenchantment, the loss of confidence in his way of life are symbolized in the opened box of silver ingots Nostromo finds. Decoud, just before his suicide, had broken into one box and taken out four silver ingots.

Why Decoud took the four ingots is not made clear. Why only four? What could he do with the four ingots on a deserted island where silver had no more value than a handful of sand? Decoud's reasons are complicated—remember, it is the crowning act of his life, the one he commits before his embrace of death. One motivation for the act seems clear: Decoud is indeed abandoning Nostromo because he believes that Nostromo, who had failed to return within a promised time, had deserted him. Unable to bear the natural simplicity and stillness of the island, the unspoken laws of nature that have no traffic with intellectual theories or ideas, Decoud turns on Nostromo. He puts Nostromo's asserted honesty to the test by leaving Nostromo the legacy of the opened box of silver. Nostromo's simplicity of response is now locked in battle with Decoud's cynicism. What will Nostromo do? Will the silver tempt him, change him as it has changed everyone else? Decoud will never know what he has accomplished, but he knows he has set things in motion.

The opened box of silver is too much temptation for Nostromo. He starts to steal the silver a little at a time. Pragmatically, he cannot achieve wealth too suddenly—an abrupt change in his style of living would cause wonder and lead to an exposure of the theft. Symbolically and psychologically, Nostromo's petty thievery is necessary in the delineation of his character. By committing petty crimes—small thefts of silver at a time—he tries to avoid the knowledge of his moral decline. By engaging in petty thievery, Nostromo, who had always quested after the heroic gesture, shrinks in stature.

The question remains: was it Decoud's wish that Nostromo fall? Full of contempt for himself and for the world, did Decoud wish to destroy the noble captain whom he admired? Decoud set up one obstacle that was impossible for Nostromo to overcome, simple and lacking in ideas of intrigue as Nostromo was. The missing four bars of silver. How could Nostromo explain that? If he brought back the remaining silver, everyone in Sulaco would believe he, Nostromo, had secreted away the four ingots. His reputation would be ruined. Nostromo decides he may as well steal the whole treasure as well as stand accused, silently, of stealing four bars of it.

In many of his works Conrad spoke of the perversion of ideas. Here is one example of it. Nostromo is not able to compete in the world of intellect. Taken out of his natural element, he loses his moral bearings. No wonder, then, Nostromo resents all those who had involved him with the silver—it destroyed him with its endless alloys of meaning and temptation.

The last part of the novel tells of Nostromo's descent from a man of honor into a thief, who returns to the island periodically to steal another bar of silver. Inwardly and outwardly he has become a shadow of his former self, stealing into the night, now crouching instead of strutting, preferring to hide in the dark rather than to be, as in the old days, the center of all eyes in the open marketplace.

When a lighthouse is erected on the island, the visits of the thief become more dangerous: the likelihood of his being seen and exposed is greater. Manning the lighthouse is Nostromo's old friend Viola. (Both Nostromo and Viola are Italians who in some aspects represent the spirit of Garibaldi in his revolt in the nineteenth century for Italy's freedom and unity.) Nostromo becomes engaged to Viola's older daughter, Linda, but he loves the younger daughter, Gisella. As Viola sees it, the younger daughter is pretty and will have suitors; the older daughter is plain and needs a father to marry her off.

Viola suspects Gisella has a lover because of her disappearances from the house. One night when Nostromo steals to his treasure (now the treasure is both the silver and his secret meetings with Gisella), Viola encounters and shoots him. Viola believes he is acting honorably, protecting his daughter from the lover stealing to meet her. Only after he has fired the fatal shot does he realize he has killed his oldest and truest friend. The irony is blatant—the thief murdered for a theft other than the one committed.

Before Nostromo dies, he pleads to see Mrs. Gould. She is the one person in whom he has continued to retain his belief of purity of conduct, of faith in the ideals of high personal conduct. He confesses his lie, and offers to tell her the hiding place of the silver. She advises him to take the secret with him to the grave. "No one misses it now. Let it be lost forever."

Like Marlow in *Heart of Darkness*, Mrs. Gould prefers to keep others in a world of illusion. She will protect Nostromo's good name. The ending of *Heart of Darkness* and *Nostromo* bear this similarity: the final comment is that of the necessity of sustaining illusion. In *Heart of Darkness* it was the woman who needed to be kept in illusion, whose world would crumble if the truth were told. Marlow does not tell the truth, does not shatter the "universe" of the girl. In *Nostromo* it is the woman who knows the truth and who will keep secret about it. Mrs. Gould tells the dying Nostromo, "I, too, have hated the idea of that silver from the bottom of my heart." She is realistic enough, however, to know that one cannot escape from the greed that is as characteristic of man as his belief and illusion in the pursuit of honor. For Mrs. Gould—for all those strong enough to bear it—the truth is evident: the "silver" is at the bottom of everything, of Mrs. Gould's knowledge, Nostromo's reputation, Decoud's death, Gould's autistic involvement with it, Dr. Monygham's restless journey between misanthropy and optimism, Sotillo's savagery, and Montero's greed. Silver, which is an incorruptible metal, corrupts all those who touch it.

Nostromo is divided into three parts. Each part has at the center one of the three main characters. Part I is dominated by Charles Gould and the mine. Indeed, "silver" is found in the first and last sentences of the novel.

Gould is an idealist who believes that progress, advanced civilization, and general improvement of man's state follow from an industrialized society. Completely absorbed in the operation of his mine, Gould is as hard-working, dedicated, and virtuous as any of Conrad's sea heroes. He has few intellectual interests (politics and economics interest him merely as factors affecting the operation of his mine), and he appears simple and undemanding. His flesh is thin, as if he has renounced the feast of life. His asceticism is that of the missionary technocrat. His wife, Mrs. Gould, by contrast, is heavier; she contains *flesh* and life. She fills a room whereas Gould seems diminished, a fragment in any place but at his mine or on his horse directing the workers of the mine. Mrs. Gould is understanding about the diminution of her life as wife, mother, and lover. They have no children, for Gould can conceive of none, neither think nor feel about human children, because the mine is his child, it requires all his care. Thus Mrs. Gould begins to treat her husband as child-lover, mothering and protecting him against the possibilities of loss of his cherished illusions.

In some ways Gould resembles in temperament Captain MacWhirr and the Marlow of "Youth." Clearly Conrad was expressing admiration for Mac-Whirr and Marlow; clearly in the depiction of Gould he was expressing an ironic despair. What is the essential difference between these two types of character? Mac-Whirr could say he did not care what flag his ship sailed under so long as it was commanded well and faithfully. Gould does not care who owns the mine so long as he runs it according to principles of efficiency. Yet Conrad makes clear that once the missionary American imperialist Holroyd buys into the mine, the mine becomes a perversion of idea. The perversion is in "the idea." What "idea" has perverted Gould's idealism of hard work and "stupid and firm" faith?

Gould is a menace because he refuses to acknowledge the consequences of his avoidance of any ideas but his own; he formulates a scheme of ideas, bounded with the coating of insularism, that he calls his credo. What he will not face is that his principles merely clothe a naked disinterest in people. For example, Gould's decision to judge matters solely in terms of the mine is a political one, for the mine and its operations profoundly affect the country, and thus its political and social institutions and its liberties and customs. The mine then becomes an impersonal force, a symbol of the capitalistic enterprise and of its impersonal morality. The rules of capitalism—that is, the workings of the mine—are indifferent to humanity; the only measure they engage in is a technocratic one, a standard of efficiency.

Nostromo, who is at the center of the third and longest part of the novel, has been compared to Gould in that both are childlike men, moved by one or two ideals to which they hold firm. Each is apolitical. Their interest is in personal conduct reflecting their visionary ideals. Nostromo could join either the rebels or the established government forces in the Occidental Province. He chooses the endangered established government—a progressive liberal group which, it is important to remember, came to power through rebellion against a previously established bureaucracy—because his friends are in Sulaco. Nostromo wants only to be brave and fearless, to indulge his appetite for action and honor, and to hear the shouts of praise of his countrymen. Gould misleads Nostromo, for he obliges him to act on the premise that the silver is essential to the progress of Costaguana, and of all primitive peoples. Gould takes a simple man and infects him with the idea of conversion to the religion of silver. He makes of Nostromo a soldier in the imperialist cause. Gould's proselytizing of Nostromo is a corruption as thoughtless as Gould's own imperious idealism. Believing only in the sanctity of the mine, and the progress and light it will bring, he does not concern himself with the issue of how he is inalterably affecting Nostromo's life.

Gould and Nostromo stand at each end of the novel as forces that sustained the Occidental Republic. In the center is Martin Decoud, the intellectual who conceived of the birth of that republic. At the end of the novel, Decoud's great love, the beautiful Antonia Avellanos, and her uncle, Father Corbellan, are plotting to unite the Occidental Republic with the remains of Costaguana (using exactly the same arguments Decoud had advanced for the secession of the Province). The irony of man's eternal folly in the political

—and therefore the human—arena is made manifest again.

Decoud differs from Gould and Nostromo in that he is a man of ideas. "Don Carlos [Gould] is a sensible man. It's a part of solid English sense not to think too much; to see only what may be of practical use at the moment. . . . I am clear-sighted." Decoud is essentially ideas, and the lack of body to clothe his ideas finally destroys him. (Decoud constantly expresses his love of the beautiful Antonia, but it is a curiously rationalized expression of love; physical love for Decoud, when thinking of Antonia, is always something in the future, a disembodied enchantment.) Left alone on the island with the silver, Decoud cannot bear the solitude. The man who held other men in intellectual contempt cannot exist without them as audience. The punishment inflicted on him by isolation could not be more apt, because he sees and hears his ideas come to *nothing*, mere air above a desert.

Several minor characters also reflect Conrad's views on modern politics and the human condition. Mrs. Gould makes the best of a situation that has stolen her cherished illusions from her. In recompense, she creates another, self-willed illusion, and that is in the efficacy of her acts of charity. Her idolizer, Dr. Monygham, has learned to despise mankind because under torture he had betrayed his friends. Dr. Monygham cannot forgive himself until Mrs. Gould provides a bridge to his rescue through her belief in him. Together the two run a hospital in Sulaco. Dr. Monygham forces himself to believe in the possibility of a better earth. He knows life is based on lies; even in his "redemption" he is living a lie, the harboring of doubt about his benefactor's philosophy. He goes on with his welfare work because he is terrified that he will lose Mrs. Gould's support if he admits to his lack of faith. It is Mrs. Gould's personal friendship, her presence and supportiveness, that sustain Monygham, not her beliefs. Yet she insists on Monygham's allegiance to those beliefs, or at least the good doctor fears she does.

Conrad once wrote: "since from the duality of man's nature and the competition of individuals, the life-history of the earth must in the last instance be a history of a really very relentless warfare." These words describe the constancy of his observations on human nature, the endless battle between idealism (and illusion) and pessimism (and paralysis). Costaguana, which can be literally translated as the coast of bird excrement (*guano* is the Spanish word for bird excrement), is the land where the ideals of politics are celebrated and malpracticed, where the high-sounding phrases of Don Jose Avellanos and his philosophy of rationalism as well as the drippings of peasant bandits, such as the Montero brothers, exist side by side (their drippings, Conrad images up, carry the odor of bird excrement). The island off the coast of Costaguana, where Martin Decoud, the most intellectual character in all of Conrad's work, commits suicide, is a refuge for bird excrement: the only living matter on it are birds, and a bird of prey waits for Martin to die.

Conrad called *Nostromo* one of his two greatest novels. It represents his most conscious use of technique. No one of his other novels is as complex. With all its intellectual, theoretical discussion of politics and the motives of men, it remains a novel of characters in action.

Although it is highly complicated in structure, and although the composition of it put Conrad under an enormous nervous strain—he told his friend R. B. Cunninghame-Grahame that he was "dying over that curst *Nostromo* thing"—it was written in great passion, and its completion in two years is a remarkable feat. The novel was inspired by a circumstance of the kind

Conrad liked to ascribe to the "inscrutability" of the universe. In a book he casually purchased, Conrad read an account of a theft of silver and was reminded of a seaman he had known in his youth. Instinctively Conrad knew that the man described in the book and the seaman he had known were one and the same thief. From this simple beginning the enormous complex of the novel spread its ways. From the inspiration of a lowly robbery, Conrad created a mirror of moral and political thievery in the Western world.

Some critics have charged Conrad with a loss of style in the third part of the novel, a strain in writing evidenced by Conrad's heaping up of adjectives. Part of this stylistic failure has been attributed by at least one critic to Conrad's fatigue in the sheer act of completing the work. It is true that the writing in the third section is florid and rhetorical, filled with abstract nouns and noun phrases, but the power of the whole novel overrides any of its particular faults. One of these faults, a fault found in the work of many profound writers, is that instead of resolving matters in the concluding pages, Conrad found still more questions to ponder.

For example, one of the brilliant and mystifying touches is the appearance of the "pale photographer, small, frail, blood-thirsty, the hater of capitalists," in the hospital where Nostromo is dying. The photographer is the last person to speak to Nostromo before his death. Conrad's description of the scene, brief and cold in tone, suggests a number of meanings. The photographer, who suspects the silver did not sink to the bottom of the ocean, tries to steal the secret of the silver's hiding-place. The photographer alludes to the necessity of money for those who fight the rich.

It is ironic that both the rich (the Goulds) and the poor (the photographer) claim Nostromo for their own purposes, and are willing to manipulate him through appeals to his honor and his vanity, but that Nostromo never truly belongs to any group. All, Conrad may be saying, are playing a game, even Nostromo after he has succumbed to the perversion of human nature in the conquest of spontaneity through dogma and greed. Nostromo's final comment, his comment on humanity and the tricks played on it, arises from the encounter with the photographer. The photographer, who assumes Nostromo is one of the group of men, like the photographer himself, out to destroy capitalism, asks, "Comrade Fidanza [Nostromo], you have refused all aid from that doctor [Monygham]. Is he really a dangerous enemy of the people?" Conrad describes Nostromo's response: "In the dimly lit room Nostromo rolled his head slowly on the pillow and opened his eyes, directing at the weird figure perched by his bedside, a glance of enigmatic mocking scorn. Then his head rolled back, his eyelids fell, and the capataz of the cargadores died without a word. . . ."

That scene, like so many in Conrad's works, puzzles and enriches the reader. It illuminates for the reader the elusiveness of Conrad's art, an art which is tantalizing because it is elusive and beckoning, meeting its promise of light, but also constantly suggesting a further meaning, a newer horizon beyond the one seen, a sense of the mystery and resolution of human character. *Nostromo* for these reasons remains one of the most extraordinary works in English literature.

6

Exiles and Untouchables:
The Secret Agent
and *Under Western Eyes*

Conrad's contemporaneity is nowhere more evident than in *The Secret Agent*. In the edition of a New York newspaper one day in August 1974, there were these stories: a dynamite bomb found in the Meditation Room of the United Nations headquarters in New York; bomb blasts of nonmilitary targets in Northern Ireland; the arrest of three members of an extreme right-wing organization in Italy on charges of planting and setting off the bomb that killed twelve people in a tourist train in northern Italy; a bomb explosion at Los Angeles Airport in which two persons were killed and thirty-six injured; and the discovery of an unexploded pipe bomb at a General Motors Corporation office in Burlingame, California.

A few weeks earlier than that day in August (the date is chosen arbitrarily since in any one day during the summer of 1974, bombs as punishment for "crimes of society" were exploding all over the world), there were other stories of individuals and groups taking the law into their hands. A bomb exploded in the Tower of London, where a large number of Scandinavian and German tourists had come to view the historic display of Anglo-Saxon weaponry. A month earlier a blast ripped apart the Los Angeles headquarters of the state attorney general. Terrorism by kidnapping was also part of daily life. Hostages were seized by revolutionary groups to bring attention to their cause, to make a complacent public aware of the purported crimes they were allowing the forces of tyranny and repression to perpetrate.

The employment of violence is not a new phenomenon. Examples in earlier history of violence as symbol abound, but the twentieth century has excelled in the impersonality of its acts and in the rationalization of violence. In *The Secret Agent* Conrad created an archetype of the modern era, the amoral scientist, the technocrat above and beyond morality and thus dispossessed of it in his portrait of the Professor and his bomb. The bomb was the closest thing to the Professor's heart; he carried it in his pocket wherever he went; it nourished him, he fondled it. He loved it as he loved no other thing, for he had created it out of his own cold passion. It was perfect. He despised humanity because it was imperfect.

It is of course difficult to write a comedy about such horrendous matter, but perhaps the only way to keep one's sanity in the face of technocracy without countervailing morality is to portray the situation in all its absurdities and in all the blackness of its comedy. To keep the blackness from overwhelming him, to express his view that the world of *The Secret Agent* is composed of the aridity of reason without the passion of humanism, Conrad portrayed that world in satiric vision. Almost every moment in *The Secret Agent* is a moment of ironic comment. The world is turned upside down, because that is Conrad's comment on the world he is portraying. It has been stood on its head, allowed to become absurd, because "ideas"—or ideology—has perverted its balance. Conrad in his bitter irony lacerated the right-wing extremists as well as the left-wing theorists; he was searching for the common cause, but in the London of his secret agent, commonality had given way to specialized groups each battling for its definition of justice and its right to administer that justice in its chosen way.

Conrad's irony in this novel is of a special sort, the irony of a bitter wit who tears away the veils of illusion. There is mocking laughter in the novel—it is the sound of someone trying to draw attention to the terrors of twentieth-century political life. There is distance, there is control, for Conrad's irony provides him with a base from which to shoot at his targets.

Nothing is as it seems in *The Secret Agent*. The most simple things turn out, on Conrad's examination, to be shaky complexities. Verloc, the central character in the novel, if there is to be one, or perhaps only a cog in the anarchist underground, is a triple agent who works as a spy for a reactionary foreign government and as a member of an underground anarchist organization. Also a police informer, he runs a pornography shop on one of London's dark streets. (The idea of a man using a pornography shop as a coverup for his illegal activities has its comic point, but it is as well a symbolic representation of the dissembling world of the characters.)

Verloc's wife, Winnie, is unaware of her husband's role as espionage agent, and although she probably knows what is going on in the pornography shop, she pretends an ignorance. The truth is, Winnie Verloc prefers to be kept in the dark—some things, for her, do not bear much "looking into." Conrad is expressing an irony in his delineation of Winnie's "stupid and firm" insistence on not seeking after unpleasant things. Whereas her husband has his feet in so many doors he can only lumber around, she, in her limited perspective of family loyalty and duty, is one of the few characters in the novel to show real passion and common courtesy.

Verloc has redeeming qualities: he assumes financial support for his wife's idiot brother and her ailing mother, he makes few demands of Winnie except she be a dutiful wife and remain ignorant of his affairs. Such qualities are hardly "redeeming" in the heroic or tragic sense. They are attributes of redemption in the comedy of life; comedies are not filled with noble heroes but with pathetic and sometimes lovable ones.

At the opening of the novel, Verloc is on his way to the embassy of the reactionary foreign government, where he will be berated by the chief officer, Mr. Vladimir. Mr. Vladimir spends half the interview with Verloc denouncing him for his obesity: a man of the people, an anarchist, should be lean and hungry. Vladimir, himself a well-fed reactionary, is elegantly thin.

Mr. Vladimir's aim, as representative of his government, is the destruction of the inimical international anarchist movement. Anarchists in England are more dangerous than elsewhere, Vladimir reasons, because England, with her traditions of democratic guarantees and personal liberty, allows the free movement of anarchist groups and the dissemination of their literature. Vladimir suggests that Verloc arrange for the bombing of the Greenwich Observatory, and lay the blame for the act on the anarchists.

It is interesting that Conrad, with his notions of the fluidity of time, his consciousness of time as a continuous present rather than a progressive, historic order, chose the Greenwich Observatory, which measures and catalogues time, as his symbolic object for bombing. Time will not stop, Vladimir argues, but a blow will have been struck at science (and perhaps for Conrad the science of measuring time?). *Science is the fetish of the twentieth century*, the embassy chief declares. Art and morality and religion have lost their appeal with the masses. To arouse people, one must hit at their sacred passions and rituals, and the infatuation with science is the greatest obsession of twentieth-century man.

Conrad pokes fun at the members of the anarchist group as they meet one night in the back of Verloc's shop. Yundt, the "tiger" of the movement, has always dreamed of "a band of men absolute in their resolve to discard all scruples in the choice of means, strong enough to give themselves frankly the name of destroyers, and free from the taint of that resigned pessimism which rots the world." In truth, Yundt is toothless, and depends on his secretary to help him on and off buses (a dependence he finds abhorrent). Michaelis, a thin waif when he entered prison, has emerged from those cells of deprivation a fat, flabby, almost cuddly middle-aged cherub. What was Michaelis's crime? He was a young idealist who joined in a robbery attempt engineered by an anarchist group. The plan misfired, and Michaelis, who had no clear idea of what was happening or that a victim had been shot in the attempted robbery, stepped in front of a police van and was apprehended immediately. Dazed, and still blinking (an innocent who had not learned to see things as they are), he was sentenced amid a flurry of newspaper headlines that described him as a dangerous, homicidal terrorist.

The other anarchist to attend the meeting that night is Comrade Ossipon, a young, handsome, ex-medical student, who has been a petty salesman all his life: he sells his body and his charms, or the promise of them, to sentimental and lusting women.

The talk of the anarchists becomes so violent that Winnie's idiot brother Stevie is driven to panic. Trying to control his anxiety, Stevie draws circles furiously with his pencil. Winnie takes away the carving knife with which he has been sharpening his pencil, and after the talk has excited him, with which he has been toying. Stevie's drawing of the circles stand as documentation of his artistic temperament. When Ossipon treats them with sneering rejection, Conrad symbolizes the rejection

of art by the modern, technological spirit. Throughout
the novel, Stevie, in spite of his intellectual shortcom-
ings, is depicted as being closer to the humanistic spirit
than the intellectualizing anarchists led by their belief in
science.

The carving knife, Conrad suggests, is connected
with Winnie's one passion—her love of a penniless
young butcher. Because she felt it unfair to saddle the
young man with the responsibility of providing for her
idiot brother and ailing mother, Winnie rejected his
proposal of marriage. Instead, she married Mr. Verloc,
for whom she holds simply a deep regard. The irony of
circumstance that will break Winnie's heart follows
from this beginning: for Mr. Verloc, the man Winnie
chooses as provider for her family and for whom she
sacrifices her romantic passion, hands the idiot boy the
bomb to blow up the Greenwich Observatory. Instead,
it explodes in Stevie's hands as he stumbles on a tree
root. When Winnie learns of her husband's role in her
brother's death, she experiences deep emotion for the
second time: she kills her husband with the carving
knife that Stevie had used, that butchers use in their
trade.

It is in the fourth chapter that Conrad's experi-
mentation with time takes place. The events narrated in
this chapter occur a month after the events described in
the first three chapters. The Professor (whom the
reader meets for the first time) and Ossipon sit in a
cafe discussing the death of Verloc, whom they mistakenly believe has been killed in the abortive bombing of
the Greenwich Observatory. They assume Verloc had
gone alone to the Observatory and been blown to bits
outside it. Thinking of a way to insinuate himself into
Winnie's affections now she is a widow—and thinking
more of Winnie's secret wealth than of her innate
charm (all the anarchists believe Verloc had secreted a
hoard of cash)—Ossipon goes to the Verloc shop. He

finds Winnie outside, distraught at her commission of murder of her husband. Ossipon thinks she is talking about Verloc's death in the bombing at the Observatory, information that has just been made known, and which he and the Professor had discussed; Winnie thinks Ossipon is expressing sympathy about Verloc's death because of concern for her fate (though she cannot understand how Ossipon should know about it).

Ossipon, after he has been able to piece the truth together, convinces her to go away with him. Winnie, thinking Ossipon loves her, follows him to an English Channel boat. Before the boat leaves, Ossipon scurries on shore with all the money Winnie has been carrying, the hoard that Verloc had amassed over the years and had been planning to use for his flight from his life as espionage agent. Ossipon now has a small fortune in cash. But the guilt and shame he feels at having abandoned Winnie leads him to drown himself in alcohol.

The Professor—the last image in the novel: "a pest in the street full of men"—is a very special anarchist. He lives for his dream, a perfect bomb. He carries his bomb on his person; he and the bomb are one. On a practical level, the Professor has a rationale for himself as bomb-carrier: no policeman will dare to arrest him out of fear of being blown up. Perhaps. Conrad does not make clear whether the Professor is bombast or coward. What he does convey is that the Professor is pure science without humanity. The Professor says of himself with "scientific insight" that he is "seriously ill." Conrad ends his tale with the Professor walking the streets, "frail, insignificant, shabby, miserable—and terrible in the simplicity of his idea calling madness and despair to the regeneration of the world." No one looked at the Professor as he passed by. The Professor strolled among the crowd, "unsuspected and deadly."

Although political anarchy is the narrative means

by which Conrad moves his story, the concern is with moral anarchy. As Conrad viewed the modern world, morality does not inform the political arena, and this lack vitiates the force of politics. Lack of morality, like the Professor's plague of impartial scientism, infests the entire world body. In Conrad's analysis of the modern condition, the police are just as criminal as the anarchists and political rebels, the utopians as self-interested as tyrants. Inspector Heat, an old hand in the service, uses Verloc as his informer, and sees no dereliction of duty in such an approach to his job. The Assistant Commissioner, new to the force, protects the anarchist Michaelis because Michaelis's patron, a wealthy and eccentric lady, is a friend of the Commissioner's wife; besides, the wealthy lady has influence in high places. Heat and the Assistant Commissioner spy on each other. Sir Ethelred, the cabinet minister in charge of security matters, is more interested in fisheries than in people, while his secretary, the effeminate Toodles, has other matters on his mind than the morality of government. The world then is corrupt. Each time one attempts to find a moral base, the base slips away like quicksand. Nothing is what it seems. The secret agent's secret, the message he has been bringing and to which no one listens, is that all are lying, all are playing a game. When the game overtakes the players, it is too late for the players to change the rules. They become their own victims.

  The Secret Agent has been criticized for its cynicism and sordidness. The second charge is easy to dismiss. In his Author's Note to the novel, Conrad admitted to a concern over certain possible and already-expressed objections to the novel. He claimed the "sordid surroundings and the moral squalor of the tale" were only one part of the novelistic portrait. "The whole treatment of the tale, its inspiring indignation and underlying pity and contempt, prove my detachment from the squalor and sordidness which lie simply in the outward circumstances of the setting." Even here he is protesting too much. His sense of taste is more fastidious than his readers'. The first charge—that of an irony bordering on cynicism—requires a more extensive defense, though Conrad would have to be vindicated in any court of literature. Conrad is not being cynical. He is attacking extremism, any philosophy that in its revelatory or repressive excesses, denies freedom to the nonconformist and the eccentric. He is especially wary of revolution since he feels it to be a wheel that returns to the same base with a different driver. But he is not cynical. The pain he felt prevented him from giving up on humanity.

Perhaps the best way to describe Conrad is to call him a conservationist of the moral response in politics. *The Secret Agent* and *Under Western Eyes*, the novel that followed it in publication, represent Conrad's fear of amorality and impersonality in modern life. In *The Secret Agent* only three characters possess traits that can rescue humanity from its flight into impersonality and the fetishism of science—Winnie, her mother, and her idiot brother. The mother is too old and infirm to affect the world, and she retires from it into an institution. Stevie lacks the intelligence to complement his humanity. Winnie, not possessed of extraordinary courage or intelligence, tries to keep her world intact by ignoring what cannot "bear looking into." When the world intrudes its ugliness on her, she commits murder and suicide.

Conrad's compassion shows through in his attitude toward his adopted country, England. The English, the Professor says, are willing to blind themselves to ugliness. They prefer illusion because it makes the world more fitting to them. They prefer the "idealistic conception of legality," which, along with their "scru-

pulous prejudices," is fatal to the work of revolutionists. The Professor says that the anarchists (but he
means all revolutionists) cannot survive the liberal
climate in England. Conrad's evaluation of his adopted
country places the insulated illusion of English people
—a quality of sentiment he often gives to his "stupid
and firm" characters—above the evil of dehumanization
that characterizes individuals and groups from European nations.

In Conrad's dedication of the novel to H. G. Wells
lies another key to his attitude to the underground he
has imaged up. Conrad genuinely liked Wells, though
he disliked Wells's optimism and feared the influence of
that once-popular writer on modern society. In calling
Wells on the dedication page, "The Historian of the
Ages to Come," Conrad was exhibiting the first of the
many ironies to be found in the book. He was saying
that the impersonality of science and the chaos of anarchy were, unless checked, the forces of "the Ages to
Come." Wells, Conrad believed, was in the forefront of
writers and intellectuals who were prophesying the
perfectability of mankind and social institutions
through science. The utopian socialist dream of Wells
was for Conrad a nightmare, not because of "the idea
behind it"—the goal of presumed benefit for humanity
—but because Conrad believed that any ideology
dehumanized human beings who rigidly applied its
tenets. Conrad, envying Wells's energy but despising
Wells's view of life, wrote him, "You don't care for
humanity, but think they are to be improved. I love
humanity, but know they are not."

The underground world of *The Secret Agent* is
black but human comedy. The laughter is critical: we
are, Conrad is saying, all of us in the same boat, left
and right, up and down, intellectual and idiot. In this
novel Conrad is at ease in the presentation of his ma-

terial. No strain is evident in the ending of it—one of the few times this can be said of a Conrad novel. This fact alone, this absence of felt fatigue in summing up his imponderables, makes of the work a shaped and instructive comedy about the foibles of social men. Because of its ease of style and its perfection of sustained irony, *The Secret Agent* is, as Conrad said, one of his two greatest books.

In *The Secret Agent* and his following novel *Under Western Eyes,* Conrad immerses himself in the world of revolutionists. In both novels the central character commits a crime and hopes to flee from sentence of guilt. In both novels the same question, "Where to?" is asked, a question that shows Conrad's awareness of the agonizing dilemma of conscience and self-interest. In *The Secret Agent* Inspector Heat hopes that Verloc will clear out of the country before he, Verloc, is exposed and the "system" of informer activity is uncovered. Verloc, who has just, unintentionally, led his lamblike brother-in-law to slaughter, "snarls" back: "Where to?" He knows that there is no place that will shield him from the awful knowledge of his betrayal of trust of people who treated him as friend.

Little is made of "Where to?" in *The Secret Agent,* and it is possible that the question remained to plague and intrigue Conrad into the profound exploration he gives it in *Under Western Eyes.* It is a question put in different terms in Conrad's earlier novel of flight, *Lord Jim,* when Captain Brierly, the judge at Jim's hearing, wants Jim to flee because the truth of Jim's cowardice is too unpleasant to contemplate. In *Under Western Eyes* the hero Razumov tells the interlocutor of his conscience, Inspector Mikulin, that he wants to "retire." Mikulin, knowing the impossibility of execution of such a wish, quietly asks him, "Where to?"

Razumov, in a romantically futile gesture, moves to the door of their room of inquiry, but he is too stunned by the truth of the question to leave.

In *Under Western Eyes* things are set in motion by one of those ironies common in the history of human affairs. Perhaps, even absurdity is not too strong a word. Razumov, a conscientious university student, who stays pretty much to himself, is mistakenly credited as a revolutionist by the anarchist group at the university. The assumption—or mis-assumption—comes as a result of Razumov's isolation from the general student life, and from Razumov's obviously superior intelligence and cool detachment. The true reason for Razumov's detachment is that he wants no part of turmoil or agitation. An orphan, he is searching for a place in society; he wants to become a part of the academic establishment in order to have a "home" base.

Haldin, an idealistic revolutionary who believes that terrorism and murder are acceptable tools in the struggle against imperialism and government oppression, assassinates an important Czarist official. In his flight from the scene, Haldin impulsively decides to run to Razumov's apartment, which is nearby. Haldin asks Razumov to make arrangements with the peasant Ziemanivich for a horse. Razumov goes to the peasant's quarters, but Ziemanivich is consumed in an alcoholic stupor and will not respond to Razumov's urgings.

Conrad employs all his talent for sensory appeal in this nighttime scene. Above Razumov is an endless black sky lit up by the "sumptuous fire of the stars." Beneath him is the soil of Russia on which he is stamping. He is utterly without the distraction of sound; all he can hear in the silence is the trembling of his soul. Around him is spread all of the Russia he loves, but Razumov knows he is now truly separated from it, or from his youthful vision of the fatherland and his place in it: a respected seat in society, a place in the academic profession, the gathering of scholarly awards. He knows instinctively that he cannot commit himself to Haldin and revolution, not beyond the one act in which he has failed—that of arranging a means of escape for Haldin. He knows that he is going to betray Haldin, and that he will not be able to rest anymore.

After his betrayal of Haldin to the police, Razumov is put under surveillance, and any lingering hopes of returning to "normal" life are shattered when Razumov finds his journals have been seized. At this point Razumov is allowed to leave Russia, but the price he pays for his "freedom" to emigrate is an agreement to work for the Russian secret police as a spy on the exile movement in Geneva.

Once in Geneva, Razumov finds himself a part of the Russian colony. There he meets Haldin's sister and mother, and several members of the exiled Russian revolutionary groups. Among them are the exploitative Peter Ivanovich, who has capitalized on years spent in prison by writing a book on his captivity and becoming wealthy and famous in the bargain; the savage terrorists Necator and Laspara; the devoted Tekla; and the ardent Sophia Antonovna.

Sophia Antonovna tells Razumov at one point to stop railing at fate. His constant expression of futility, she points out, is destructive to the revolutionary movement and to himself. Sophia's declaration is a key in the novel, for she speaks the truth about Razumov, but it is not the whole truth. Doubt and despair have indeed paralyzed Razumov and destroyed his ability to enjoy any activity. Doubt and pessimism are also his defense against the pain of his shattered illusions.

Razumov, as Sophia becomes aware, is a familiar modern hero: the man of isolation afflicted with the wound of paralysis, the intellectual who is deracinated by too much reasoning. (His name, in the Slavic language, means *reason*.) Even his parentage is shrouded in mystery. When Haldin seeks him out for shelter, Razumov feels life is going to deprive him of his fatherland as it has already deprived him of his parents. He feels unworthy of people's trust and love because he feels himself unworthy. To mask his desire for a love he has denied himself, Razumov holds himself above people, pretending and assuming an intellectual contempt.

Razumov is finally able to end his isolation, to begin the expiation of his guilt through a confession to Natalia, Haldin's sister. She in her saintly way forgives him and tells him she is returning to Russia to continue her brother's work. She is not paralyzed by the awareness of man's inhumanity.

Razumov must however go one step further in his journey to salvation—he must reveal to the revolutionary terrorists in Geneva his betrayal of Haldin. After hearing Razumov's confession, Nikita, one of the group, rains blows at Razumov's ears while the others hold him down. Rendered deaf by the assault, Razumov decides to return to Russia, where he will be tended by Tekla, whose self-appointed role is to take care of the sick and wounded. The novel ends with a pathetic image: the deaf Razumov nursed by a woman whose life has consisted of taking care of those injured in the revolutionary struggle.

More than any other work Conrad wrote, *Under Western Eyes* draws on the imagery of sound. At the end of the third part of the novel, Razumov in an attempt to find inner peace, goes to a wooded lake near Geneva. He stands near a statue of Rousseau, another exile from tyranny. He realizes that the only sound to which he can listen with pleasure—that of the cool wind—is foreign to human passions: "All other sounds of this earth brought contamination to the solitude of a soul." To return him to the community of people, and to end his isolation, Conrad chooses an ironic punishment. By taking away his disdain, his pride of with-

drawal from the human lot, by humbling him through
physical pain and beating, and, finally, deafness, Conrad brings Razumov into the abode of mankind. He,
who could never bear to be touched and who could not
listen to human beings (except Natalia) without contempt, is punished/freed by the loss of Natalia's kindness, the punitive strike of Nikita's blow to his ears,
and after the denouement of his journey, the touch of
Tekla's gentle care.

Conrad's novel and its paralytic hero have often
been compared to the work of Dostoievsky, a writer
Conrad read, and whose emotionality and mysticism he
feared and berated. There is little question both writers
are dealing with existential moments, and the consequences of those moments, and with passionate in-
quiries into the mystique of the Russian soul. Both
writers are dealing with crime—more the crime of
conscience than crime defined by law—and expiation
of those crimes. But Conrad, as he often protested, was
not a brother of Dostoievsky. He was not a Russian, as
he bitterly reminded his critics by referring them to the
Czarist subjugation of his native land.

In *Under Western Eyes* Conrad makes the distinction between him and Dostoievsky clearer, though he
cannot wholly deny their kinship in the exploration of
the Slav character. (Here again Conrad might object to
the inclusion of Pole in the Slavic family, for Conrad,
particularly in his later years, saw Poland as the last
frontier of Western Europe.) The distinction is realized
in the characterization of the professor of Western languages, who narrates the novel. The professor, though
he knows words—the words of the Russian language—
admits his inability to know the Russian soul. Unlike
Conrad in many ways, the professor suggests his creator in the manner of his fascination with the Russian
mind and soul. Conrad and the professor are constitu-
tionally unable to surrender themselves to mysticism.

Dostoievsky in his search for knowledge came to the doors of revelation; Conrad cannot surrender to the apocalyptic vision, and so, like the professor of Western languages, Conrad can never penetrate the mystery of the Russian soul.

The professor, who tells the tale from Razumov's journals and from his recollections of meetings with Razumov and Natalia, also signifies Conrad's awareness of his need to "distance" material. The professor removes the story, in effect, from a first-hand, immediate present tense to that of a recollection of past experience. In addition the professor is an "outsider," an exile from the group he is describing.

On one level Conrad's novel is an attempt to come to terms with the conflicts within him raised by his renunciation of his native country and by his decision to become a naturalized citizen of England. His letters reveal the agony those conflicts engendered in him, and the particular anguish he felt when Polish critics called him a deserter. While the novel has its source in this deepest part of Conrad's sensibility, there were two incidents that sparked an immediate response in Conrad and provided the shape of the work. The assassination scene, in which a high government official is killed by a student, was inspired by Conrad's reading of the newspaper accounts of the assassination of de Plehve, the Russian minister of the interior, in 1904. Conrad's visit to Geneva with his ailing son Borys in 1907 also set off a catalytic chain of memories and associations of his earlier visit to that city, when he had been hospitalized and alone, depressed and unsure of himself, an exile in all senses. That sense of exile came flooding back when he walked along the lake and saw hosts of revolutionary exiles, dreaming their dreams of return to homeland.

The ending of *Under Western Eyes*, in which Conrad was exorcising his own conflicts about divided loyalties and group allegiances, has an air of catharsis about it. In this novel about exiles, Conrad was able to close the circle of doubt and pain about his own identity. Instead of a sense of human loneliness and alienation, the novel in its purity of tragic response expresses a limited hope that man through slow progress will attain to humanism.

7

The Early
and Late Work

Conrad's greatest works were written in what may be
called his middle period—the years between 1900 and
1914. His early works bear signs of the distinction that
was to come, and in at least one of them, *The Nigger of
the Narcissus*, Conrad achieved that sense of profound
ambiguity characteristic of his strongest work.

His first novel, *Almayer's Folly*, published in
1895, is an exploration, physical and psychological, of
a man who goes through life in the most abject apathy.
Redemption for Almayer would be a turning-away
from the pits of self-pity and morbidity, an action that
Almayer can no longer effect. Almayer, who lives in the
ruins of a house in Sambir, on the eastern coast of
Borneo, really lives on dreams. When he had first come
to the place, he had expected to make a fortune. He
sold himself for that fortune by marrying the Malay
ward of his employer, Captain Tom Lingard. Lingard,
however, went bankrupt when the secret navigational
waterways of the interior of the land on the Pantai
River were exposed to Lingard's rivals.

Almayer's complete dissolution comes with the
loss of his last dream-endeavor. Dain Maroola, a young
Bali prince, comes to Sambir to buy guns to be used by
his countrymen in their struggle to oust the Dutch. Almayer agrees to help Dain Maroola smuggle guns off
the island. His price is that Maroola help him to find

the mountain of gold Almayer believes lies in the island's interior. The plan goes awry when Maroola's
ship is scuttled in a battle with Dutch forces. Maroola
escapes and returns to Sambir. There he makes preparations for his journey back to Bali. He has really
returned to Sambir to carry off Almayer's daughter
Nina; the two are deeply in love.

Nina is another dream of Almayer. For her sake
he still clings to the dream of drawing himself up out of
the slough of his despair, of making a fortune and taking her away to the civilized states of Europe. When
Nina flees with Maroola, all of Almayer's dreams collapse, and all reason for his existence deserts him.

Nina's elopement with Maroola means, to the father, that she has rejected the values to which he has
clung, values that are intimately connected with Almayer's version of European civilization. When Nina's
Malay mother aids in her daughter's flight, Almayer
interprets the action as a double betrayal. In choosing
Maroola and in accepting the aid of her mother, Nina
has chosen the Eastern side of her, and rejected the
Western.

Having lost Nina spiritually, Almayer helps her to
leave the island (she is in hiding) and to escape from
the Dutch authorities. He rows Nina and Maroola to a
cove where they will meet a ship that will take them
away from him forever. On his return to his house,
Almayer smoothes out the footprints his daughter has
made on the sand: he wants to wipe out her presence
even on the sands of time. Later he will burn the house
in which she has lived with him. Death finally relieves
him from his pain and from the opium addiction to
which he has surrendered in the face of his pain.

Almayer's Folly reveals an incipient technique in
Conrad's arsenal of craft. In the first chapter Conrad
defines the situation—old Almayer, his river, his dream,
his daughter Nina, his shattered hopes. The chapter

closes with a tableau. In Chapter Two he moves back
in time to Almayer as a young man, and to Captain
Lingard's assistance to him. Though the conventional
flashback technique is in use here, there are hints of
what is to become one of Conrad's reflectors of attitude: that is, the fluidity between past and present, the
inchoate emotional lines that blur chronology, the
streams of thought that flood past and present alike.

In *A Personal Record* Conrad wrote: "If I had not
got to know Almayer pretty well it is almost certain
there would never have been a line of mine in print."
Conrad's admission was based, at least partly, on his
fear that he was not "inventive," and that he could not
weave plots or create characters without a strong reliance on reportorial stimulus. Conrad also feared that
his ability to respond to the provocation of sensations
received from newspaper stories, overheard conversa-
tions, and his own observations would someday exhaust
itself in a nervous tension that would render him
apathetic. Conrad referred to this fear many times in
his letters; he called it the fear of the nervous writers, a
phrase he knew from his reading of Baudelaire. His
earliest central characters, those in *Almayer's Folly* and
An Outcast of the Islands, are imaginative extrapola-
tions of this fear, portraits of men who have lost their
vitality of response.

The central interest in Conrad's second novel, *An
Outcast of the Islands*, lies in the decline of Willems, a
man also befriended by Captain Tom Lingard: Lingard
had given Willems his first job. When, however, Willems asked to be allowed to work for the banker Hudig
on shore, Lingard released him. Willems at first shone
in his work for Hudig, who promoted, then affianced the
young employee to his half-caste daughter.

An egoist, Willems is so blinded by his own ambition that he does not know until his "downfall" that his
wife is Hudig's illegitimate daughter. This blindness to

fact is significant, for it shows that Willems' downfall, like Almayer's decline, is part of a dream spawned in ignorance of reality. Willems' dream of success—financial, social, fueled by bourgeois values—is shattered with the revelation of his embezzlements, his discharge by Hudig, and a savage outburst of hatred by his wife, who momentarily glories in his shame. The fact that others do not love him, and will not make allowances for him, shocks him. Dazed, he wanders back to his first benefactor, Captain Lingard. Ever the paternalist, Lingard takes Willems under his wing again, puts him on board his ship, where he will be hidden from men's eyes, and deposits him on Sambir as Almayer's assistant.

The time-setting of *An Outcast of the Islands* is earlier than that of *Almayer's Folly*. In this novel, Almayer is a younger man who still believes in the power of the rich Captain Lingard, and who callously offers Willems no consolation. Both Willems and Almayer live in a solipsistic world. Almayer, outraged at Willems' deterioration into an unkempt, fetid jungle creature, allows his five-year-old daughter Nina to label Willems a "pig." The scene is graphically conveyed: the beaten Willems shrinking away from an arrogant Almayer while about them the braying chants of a five-year-old girl fill the air.

It is Willems who sets in motion the decline of his benefactor, Captain Lingard, by revealing Lingard's trading secret, the navigable pathway into the interior, to Lingard's rivals. After Willems' betrayal, after Lingard has come to pronounce sentence on Willems—the sentence a permanent exile in the jungle—Willems feels some catharsis. The worst moment, judgment by his "father," has passed.

The final release for Willems, as for Almayer, will be death. His wife, now hysterically seeking forgiveness from him, comes to Sambir. With Almayer's spiteful help, she finds her husband with the native girl Aissa, with whom Willems has fallen passionately in love. All four meet in a clearing in the depths of the jungle. Willems has a flickering hope he can flee his fate and begin a new life through escape from the jungle. (The irony that he is now ready to forsake Aissa, from whom he could not bear to be parted the previous day, is stunning.) Willems is shot by Aissa as he grapples with her over his pistol. It is fitting that his own pistol kills him. It is also fitting that Willems, having sunk into the jungle of emotions, a place without any clear pathway of honor and discipline, should die there.

Almayer's Folly and *An Outcast of the Islands* are adventure stories with the popular hue of exoticism. In 1896, Conrad was working on still a third novel involving Captain Tom Lingard. Characteristically the new work was searching deeper into the past of Lingard. In *The Rescue* Tom Lingard is thirty-five years old and at the height of his physical prowess and glory.

Tom Lingard is a man of power and action, but in all three novels in which he appears he is involved in failure. The failure in *The Rescue* may be attributed to a willful woman; in *An Outcast of the Islands* to an egoistic, crazed man; and in *Almayer's Folly* to shrewd European financiers who are unwilling to finance Lingard's schemes. If Lingard cannot be charged with the failure of others, he can be exposed as an egoist who does not understand the "friends" he wishes to aid. Lingard is egoist enough to believe he can help anyone. He does not accept the complexities of another man's personality, possibly because that would involve him in introspection and self-analysis.

Conrad seems to want to believe in Lingard's paternal benevolence. One of the reasons he may have had difficulties in finishing *The Rescue*—it took him more than twenty years to complete it—is that he was not willing to explore profoundly the matter of Lingard's egoistic generosity. He suffered no such problems in his dealings with Almayer and Willems—what sympathy he gave them was pity for wasted, limited men misled by illusions and sentimentality. With Lingard the portrait was not so easy to paint, since Lingard was a man of virtue. It was his virtue—his autocratic generosity and his pure, insular firmness—that led to his downfall. Conrad never faced the immensity of the problem of character in Lingard, where virtue is its own punishment as well as reward. When he finally returned to the manuscript some twenty years later he avoided the moral complexities of characterization. He even gave the novel a new name; from *The Rescuer* it became *The Rescue*. The new title moved the focus from character to the sensational aspects of romantic adventure.

In what way did Lingard frighten Conrad, frighten him enough to inhibit him? Lingard's failure in *The Rescue* is partly the result of his trust in a woman, and possibly Conrad may have had difficulty in treating such a situation in his fiction. His studies of women show a marked progression of characterization, from an uneasiness in his early work to a sentimental tribute in his last works. Women in the early books do not understand the facts of life; it is the job of men like Lingard to shelter them. By the time of *Heart of Darkness* in 1902, Conrad's women need to be protected by illusion: Marlow lies to Kurtz's fiancee in order to keep her universe from tottering. In Conrad's major work, created during his middle years, his portrayal of women is complex and deep. One element in Conrad's work remains constant: Conrad's women do not exhibit the need to "test" their dreams; they simply hold onto them.

Conrad's first long "ship" story, *The Nigger of the Narcissus*, marks his commitment to the profession of author. In the Author's Note to the 1914 American edition, Conrad wrote: "After writing the last words of that book, in the revulsion of feeling before the accomplished task, I understood that I had done with the sea, and that henceforth I had to be a writer." In this work he opened himself to material that came from the deepest recesses of his being. He concentrated on men's performance on the sea; here, he presented the skein that shows the sea as creator and destroyer, enemy and lover, the center of life and death. In Conrad's world the sea, with the ship at the center of it, offers man the opportunity to respond to the high calling of duty, fidelity to a code of honor, and a sense of responsibility to others.

Simple enough on the surface, *The Nigger of the Narcissus* has accommodated myriad critiques. On one level, it is a journey into darkness, a comedic trip in the Dantean sense that the ship survives the underworld to come home. On a straightforward narrative level the trip involves a near-mutiny, an exhibition of pity for a dying man, and a robbery that is justified by the thief on the grounds of society's mistreatment of him.

The narrator, who does not partake in the action, opens the story with a reference to the blackness that the ship must pass through. He closes the tale with a reference to the sailors as "the dark knot of seamen" drifting "in sunshine." Between these images of darkness and light the story is shaped.

At the beginning, when the ship has not yet left port—when it is still close to land—the narrator implies a certain sense of disorder: the sailors smile in "the tempest of good-humoured and meaningless curses"; they are seen in the haze of tobacco smoke. By his choice of detail, Conrad is telling the reader that the men do not yet know their *places*; they have not yet moved into functioning positions of discipline. The narrator introduces Singleton—bearded, gray, possessing the simple mind of "big children who people those dark and wandering places of the earth." Other sailors appear on deck. The narrator reserves his scorn for one of them, Donkin, whose unkempt, beggarly appearance parallels his inner state of pettiness.

The narrator makes it clear that Donkin knows how to manipulate the men. He acts out of the sure knowledge that the sailors will become touched by "their own readiness to alleviate a shipmate's misery." Their indulgence sends a "wave of sentimental pity through their doubting hearts." This rush to pity for Donkin is a foreshadowing of the men's response to the black sailor, Jimmy Wait, who is the last man to come on board ship.

Wait, who is late in reporting for duty, astounds the men and the impatient officers with his "calm, cool, towering, superb figure." He tells them: "I belong to the ship." In his first words he sums up his central role: the ship must wait for him, since he belongs to it (and therefore the ship to him); it must wait for him, as the crew will do later in the story; he is a weight that the ship must bear, a heavy weight that the crew must toss overboard if they are to survive.

Wait is dying, and his sickly presence causes a number of reactions. For Donkin, Wait is a malingerer, a more clever slacker than he, able to deceive a ship's crew. For the chief mate, Mr. Baker, Wait is a distasteful enigma. When Wait tells Mr. Baker of his illness, Mr. Baker replies, "Then why the devil did you ship on board here?" For Singleton, one of the "big children" of the world, Wait is an unpleasant and unnecessary intrusion. He tells Jimmy Wait to "get on with your dying" and not to "raise a blamed fuss with us over that job. We can't help you." But Singleton's admirably self-protective logic cannot break the spell Wait produces on the other men. They want to help and take care of him. They move him to more comfortable quarters. When the great storm breaks, the men expose themselves to danger in rescuing Wait from his cabin. After the storm abates, the narrator describes the new day as a fresh start, a rebirth: an incubus has been lifted. Yet the disease is not yet exorcised, for the crew almost come to mutiny. The captain saves the situation by his firmness of command.

Jimmy Wait dies a short time later in the presence of Donkin, who then steals his belongings. Even in death Wait is reluctant to leave the ship. The shroud covering his coffin gets caught on a nail and the coffin will not slide into the sea; the men must push the body into the sea. Almost immediately afterwards, the winds change, and *The Narcissus* sails to port.

One of Conrad's strongest condemnations in the story is the exposure of Donkin as slacker: he will not do his share on ship, where each man has his appointed duty. On land Donkin can be forgotten, absorbed in the mass of other slackers; on ship, he is a festering plague. (The narrator, in a revealing comment, calls Donkin a part of the "earth" while the other men are a part of the "sea." Interesting too is that Donkin alone, among the sailors, exhibits greed; he alone opts to leave the ship and stay on shore.)

The petty evil of Donkin can be tolerated because it can be contained. The issue is not so simple with Jimmy Wait, whose presence creates an anarchy of emotion that leads to a disfunctioning of the ship, which represents the universe in this story. The narrator earlier made it known that Donkin and Wait were "bosom friends." Donkin is the only man from whom Wait will take abuse. Conrad suggests that while the two men are outcasts—cast out from the joys and discipline of the crew—there are differences. Both represent dangers, but the dangers are different. Though there is nothing evil in Jimmy Wait, as there is in Donkin, Wait is a danger to man-made order. His presence, the pity and sympathy that his illness evokes in the men—good things in and of themselves—lead the crew into storms of emotion that disturb the performance of duty. This is the dark side of Conrad's message.

Conrad's final words in the story paint the awful knowledge and its awesome consequences: though the men who have witnessed Jimmy Wait's visitation are no longer innocent, they are not yet capable of understanding what they have suffered:

The sunshine of heaven fell like a gift of grace on the mud of earth, on the remembering and mute stones, on greed, selfishness; on the anxious faces of forgetful men. And to the right of the dark group the stained front of the Mint, cleansed by the flood of light, stood out for a moment dazzling and white like a marble palace in a fairy tale. The crew of the Narcissus drifted out of sight.

This ending is characteristic of Conrad's technical device—the use of a symbol that has been allowed to hover over the story. The Mint, which stands on the right of the sailors, in full sunlight, "a marble palace in a fairy tale," represents the financiers who control the world. Though the seamen have suffered, the financiers remain in their white marble buildings, keeping their hands clean. Of course, Conrad is being ironic here, as he will be even more so in Heart of Darkness. Conrad, then, even in this predominantly symbolic story, was commenting on the socio-political conditions of which he was a part. Always fearful of the consequences of uncontrolled emotion, of anarchy and revolution within the individual as well as in the political body, he was also keenly conscious of tyranny and suffering caused

by self-centered men. The marble palace will become
the whited sepulchre city of greed that dominates the
European capital in *Heart of Darkness*.

Conrad's later years—the time between 1915 and
1924—brought him fame and a modest fortune. In
1912, when *Chance* was published as a serial in *The
New York Herald*, and in 1913 when the novel was
issued in book form, Conrad achieved his first large
measure of popularity. The public, which had largely
ignored Conrad, suddenly began to buy *Chance*. Conrad enjoyed his new-found popularity, and, true to
character, he felt that as a writer with a popular following he had to provide moral direction for his readers. In
Victory, the novel which followed *Chance*, Conrad
speaks directly to his audience about the need to commit oneself to a responsible role in the community of
men and women. In this novel, more than in any other
work, Conrad portrayed the debilitating effect of isolation on man's spirit.

When *Victory* appeared in 1915, its title misled
some readers into believing that the book dealt with
the fighting of World War I. Conrad, in his Author's
Note, takes pains to make clear the kind of victory he is
describing: "*Victory* was the last word I had written in
peace time. It was the last literary thought which had
occurred to me before the doors of the Temple of Janus
flying open with a crash shook the minds, the hearts,
the consciences of men all over the world." *Victory*,
then, is an allegorical tale of the battle between skeptical isolationism and passionate acceptance of fellow
human beings.

The protagonist, Axel Heyst, is a middle-aged
man who has withdrawn from involvement in human
affairs. He justifies his social and personal withdrawal
in several ways. One, as a man of middle age, he has
done his duty, fulfilled his responsibilities; he has de-

manded little from others while always paying his way. Second, his father, a philosopher of skepticism, had encouraged his son to strive for intellectual distance from human commitment. Such aloofness protects a person against a world the philosopher saw as demeaning and entangling. The narrator who opens the novel says of Heyst he "was not conscious of friends or of enemies. It was the very essence of his life to be a solitary achievement, accomplished not by hermit-like withdrawal with its silence and immobility, but by a system of restless wandering, by the detachment of an impermanent dweller amongst changing scenes. In this scheme he had perceived the means of passing through life without suffering and almost without a single care in the world—invulnerable because elusive."

Heyst had committed himself first to a maritime career and then to a coal-mining venture in order to help a financially-pressed acquaintance, Morrison. When the coal-mining venture failed, Heyst was left in possession of the island on which the mine was located. At this point Heyst decides to retire from the world to this island, and live there as ruler of his hermitage. Occasionally he goes to the mainland, where he dines with another seaman, Davidson (who narrates the later part of the story). Heyst admits to some measure of kinship with this old seaman and colleague. On one of his visits, while he is staying at Schomberg's hotel, Heyst meets Lena, who is part of a musical troupe of women who solicit money from the hotel guests after their performance. Her helpless state appeals to Heyst, and he decides to help her escape with him to his island. For Lena it is an escape from the dreary, demeaning round of jobs she has held since her childhood in a gray London street shut out from the sun; it is also an escape from the looming trap of whoredom and physical enslavement Schomberg, the hotel owner, plans for her.

Heyst had been living in a world of illusion for
some time, but he does not suspect that he has chosen
illusion as a way of life. He rationalizes all his acts in a
solipsistic manner. For example, in helping Lena, he
takes no heed of the consequences, he simply acts as if
he can do his deeds, finish them off, and be done with
them. Having lived so long in isolation—spiritually
since he was a child, physically since his retreat to his
island—he believes he can arbitrarily slice off a portion
of life and have no further accounting of it. As the
narrator says of Heyst, "You don't take a woman into a
desert jungle without being made sorry for it sooner or
later, in one way or another; and Heyst being a gentleman only makes it worse."

Conrad presents Heyst's aloofness, his rationalization of intellectual distance and disdain, with sympathy,
but he is careful to show that Heyst is indeed an arbitrary man. One of Conrad's illustrations of that blindness is conveyed in several scenes in which Heyst talks
about "facts." Early in the novel, Heyst, as maritime
officer, as businessman, as skeptic, says he is interested
only in "hard facts," in "facts alone." As a result of his
demonstrative attitude, Heyst becomes known among
his associates as the "Hard Facts" man. Later, however, when Heyst is trying to save his coal mine, he tells
a friend that he is "done with facts." The change in
attitude is striking and illustrative of Heyst's arbitrary
rationalizations. As long as he is living alone, separated
from mankind, he can get away with such rationalizations; he believes in them with such force that they
become his truth. The narrator and Heyst's friend,
Davidson, use another term to describe Heyst. They
call him a romantic, tinging the world to the hue of his
temperament. As a romantic, Heyst does not see a
thing "all round, as it were." He sees what he wishes to
see.

Heyst does not realize that his rationalized way of

life—his commitment to isolation—incurs the wrath and envy of others. Schomberg, even before Heyst robs him of his desired prize Lena, hates Heyst. Heyst threatens Schomberg simply by his very being: his gentlemanly reserve is interpreted by Schomberg as a condemnation of Schomberg's vulgar activities. The hatred is so consuming that Schomberg lies to three thieves, who come as guests to his hotel, about a treasure lying in wait for plunder on Heyst's island. The three men—Mr. Jones, Ricardo, and Pedro—invade Heyst's island retreat.

The final section, and the weakest one in the novel, describes the battle between Lena and Heyst in one camp, and Jones, Ricardo, and Pedro in the other. In spite of melodramatic dialogue and a sentimentally romantic portrait of Lena, Conrad conveys some striking insights into the five allegorical figures on Heyst's island.

Jones is, like Heyst, a man in withdrawal from community. He is a criminal by habit; having no sense of wholeness he destroys, in recompense, what seems whole to him. Afraid of women because of their sexual threat to him, Jones denies his body. Jones has been called a repressed homosexual because of several details of characterization and dress: his archthinness, his penciled eyebrows, his flowered dressing robe, his abhorrence of women and physical contact with them. The sexual variance is important because it symbolizes Jones's withdrawal from society.

Jones attempts to kill Heyst, but the bullet from his gun hits Lena. Metaphorically, Jones had aimed at the feeling of love for Lena which Heyst had just acknowledged. Jones was trying to destroy such knowledge because he, an emasculated man, lacked the capacity for human love.

Lena's death is a "victory" in that she has at last committed an act for someone she loves. As her death

is an accident, Conrad may be presenting a further
irony. Did Lena die believing in an illusion, that her
sacrifice was meaningful? It is at this point that the
weakness of the novel shows through—for Lena is presented as a noble, stained woman redeemed by love for
Heyst. The rhetoric with which Conrad clothes his
description of Lena mars her portrait, and her death
scene, as Heyst lifts her in his arms, seems one out of a
storybook.

Conrad presents Lena in such a way that the
reader cannot be sure Conrad himself is not indulging
in romantic fantasy. The irony that controlled his greatest work is missing in the final section of *Victory*. The
lesson, the morality of the tale, dominates: Heyst's re-
alization of his capability for love through the knowledge he is capable of being loved. The lesson, though it
comes too late to be sweet, is clear: withdrawal as a
way of life is death to the individual and sickness to
society. This is the social message of the story, the
allegorical communication, Conrad's rendering of the
aridity of the intellect, the "dry rot" that is spreading
into twentieth-century life. It is a message later writers,
among them Ernest Hemingway, André Gide, Thomas
Mann, Graham Greene, all avid readers of Conrad, will
give to their readers.

If the sentimental portrait of Lena and the blunt-
ness of allegorical statement weaken *Victory*, they do
not rob the novel of its many triumphs. The portrait of
Axel Heyst is one of Conrad's most masterful. Axel is a
character to whom most readers respond with deep feeling. He is a noble and tragic figure whose victory over
his inhibitions comes too late for him to enjoy the fruits
of that victory. He represents some of the noblest aspects of man, but, like a tragic figure flawed by intellectual pride, he is unable to enjoy those virtues. Conrad said of Heyst in the Author's Note that in his "fine

detachment" he "had lost the habit of asserting himself. I don't mean the courage of self-assertion, either moral or physical, but the mere way of it, the trick of the thing, the readiness of mind and the turn of the hand that comes without reflection and leads the man to excellence in life, in art, in crime, in virtue and for the matter of that, even in love. Thinking is the great enemy of perfection. The habit of profound reflection, I am compelled to say, is the most pernicious of all the habits formed by the civilized man."

Conrad's words are harsh, so harsh that a reader may suspect a deep nerve has been touched in the writer. Perhaps the overstatement, the above condemnation of Heyst, written several years after the novel itself, reveals Conrad's own fears of intellectualization. In casting off Heyst in this cold manner, Conrad may be evading the skein of good and evil in all of us that Conrad's genius impelled him to paint in the portrait of Heyst. For in the novel Heyst lives as a man of many parts, even in his most unattractive moments.

Heyst, in a confession to Lena the night of her death, reveals he thought he could assume an arrogance of grace, confer salvation on another human being, and remain uninvolved: his was to be the kingdom of beneficence. Heyst was to feel the full impact of his fatal error: his end was in his isolated attempt at communication with another human being. With Morrison, a man he tried to rescue from bankruptcy, he learned he could not dismiss the gratitude of another person; he was beholden to the man, just as the man was in debt to him. With Lena, he learned he could not extend kindness without its being returned in kind. Heyst called a human tie the germ of corruption, but in his confession to Lena was he not pleading with her to nurse him through his fear of human attachment?

It is in such scenes that the majesty of Conrad's

prose reverberates. When Heyst is on stage, the novel is triumphant.

After *Victory*, Conrad seemed willing to settle for a lesser vision. Both in his writing and in his private life he seemed to become more accepting of and accepted by mankind. In his writings, that magnanimity of spirit, that mellow ease and ripening peace of age led to a number of sentimental and flabbily romantic works. Among these are *The Arrow of Gold*; the completed version of *The Rescue*; *The Rover*; and the fragment entitled "Suspense."

8

The Distance Spanned

No great writer is available for summary. A critic can
provide a view of the writer by suggesting certain lines
of development and by exploring the paths of the writer's growth and development and decline. A view of the
writer may also be attained by looking at the recurring
imagery, phrases, situations and types of character
found throughout his work. Some of these have been
described earlier. Predominant among them are Conrad's observations on illusion, the necessity that exists
for some human beings to follow their dreams to the
visionary, sometimes horrifying end of them. Conrad
also commented on the need for moderation: for most
men it is their protection against forces they cannot
understand and control. Conrad expressed admiration
for high deeds, great accomplishments; there is also in
his work the corresponding awareness that the qualities
that make for those high deeds are capable of produc-
ing crimes. The man of honor and the villain have
something in common; the heroic sea captain affirming
his responsibility for his crew and the outlaw rebelling
against society are brothers in some ways.

Conrad often presented the dual nature of man
through the technique of employing a conventional narrator to comment on the acts of an outcast or isolated
man. Not every Conradian narrator achieves flesh and
urgency. In *Chance, Under Western Eyes,* and *The*

Arrow of Gold, he is often a paper figure, a conception rather than a full-bodied creature. But in all of his appearances he is a man proud of his national and social group, tolerant of the political and social situation he is describing, and aware of the need to find a place for the man who does not fit into his society. Conrad juxtaposed the two types of figure, for each represents a complementary aspect of human nature. Marlow is a possible Jim and a possible Kurtz if he would let go; it is also impossible that Marlow could be Jim or Kurtz because what makes Marlow the man he is, is the fact that he cannot let go, that he has the control that enables him to explore with Jim and Kurtz their psychic journeys and not lose his self-control. The loss of control—Jim's desertion of the *Patna*, Kurtz's lust for ivory, Razumov's betrayal of Haldin, Nostromo's theft of silver—leads to an awareness that is not otherwise obtainable, but it also leads, and must lead in Conrad's work, to exclusion of these flawed men from society for the general good of that society.

This apparent need on Conrad's part to resolve the conflict of stability and dynamism in man's character spurred him to his greatest writing. In his search for understanding, he often used such words as facts and inscrutability. The universe remained inscrutable to him. There were times when, for him, facts lost their currency in the greater meaning of things. Yet he continued to immerse himself in the pain and effort that might lead him closer to the truth. No matter how small, how pitiably powerless his knowledge of truth might be in an alien and "inscrutable" world, Conrad sailed into his journeys of moral exploration with bravery and sincerity. He held his readers fascinated because he did not adulterate the pain of his descriptions.

Conrad stated his esthetic in his Preface to *The Nigger of the Narcissus*. Art, for Conrad, should of necessity have many meanings. It should be a provocative and suggestive haze of thought rather than a clear explication of idea. A scientist may abstract, a journalist may excerpt daily lines of activity, but an artist must convey the mystery and evocative haze of life.

Just what does Conrad mean by his notions of haze and suggestiveness? Conrad never defined such terms partly because to do so would be to negate his view of art. Art cannot be reduced; its weight is immeasurable. Conrad suggests certain meanings: the haze is to lead the viewer onto a further horizon, a deepening picture. Because the surface is not clear, it is necessary to probe deeper. Thus the haze pulls the reader in, not necessarily to light but to the possibility of it.

Conrad's humor and irony are sometimes forgotten in the face of his profound moral and esthetic stance. Some of his most brilliant literary moments are those of ironic comedy: the bitter humor of "An Outpost of Progress" (whose original title, "A Victim of Progress," more obviously presented its writer's view) in which two men die as a result of a quarrel over a lump of sugar; in "The End of the Tether," in which two men take time out from the struggle for survival in a raging storm at sea to revile each other; in *The Arrow of Gold*, in which a crazed suitor dons armor in an attempt to break down the door (the moat) his lady love hides behind; and in every moment of *The Secret Agent*, possibly the most sustained English ironic novel in the twentieth century with the exception of Ford Madox Ford's *The Good Soldier*. The scene in *The Secret Agent* in which Verloc eats his dinner after his wife has discovered he is responsible for her brother's death is a masterpiece of ridiculous logic. Verloc eats because he has exhausted himself trying to explain things to his wife. There is nothing more to say, and the food is on the table. Fittingly, if in an absurdly logical way, Verloc gets his just deserts when Winnie stabs him in passionate outrage with the butcher knife that had been used to cut the dinner meat.

Conrad's mastery of irony serves to explain part of the fascination he has exerted on the Western world. Ernest Hemingway chose Conrad as a mentor because Conrad's extraordinary plunge into the psychic underworld of men was the guideline for Hemingway's own journeys into awareness of self. Conrad's impressionistic style of shifting viewpoint and chronology, and his explorations into the divided selves of his isolated heroes, influenced William Faulkner's work. Faulkner found in Conrad the patterns he would use of never-ending circles in which identity and light merged and broke with illusion and blackness. André Gide's interest in Conrad is attested to by the fact that he translated Conrad's *Typhoon*. The circling method—the angling-in of viewpoint and the repetition of motifs—that today is familiar in the work of such different writers as Saul Bellow, Vladimir Nabokov, Anthony Burgess, and Juan Luis Borges—was developed and channeled into new streams of prose by Conrad as well as by the two other writers usually associated with modern experimental writing, James Joyce and Virginia Woolf. T. S. Eliot and Graham Greene have proclaimed their debt to Conrad in his emphasis on moral force, an emphasis that influenced and shaped their own work.

Two puzzling aspects of Conrad continue to tantalize his readers. Neither his biography nor his work reveals the answer to the questions of why he had so much difficulty with the conclusions of his novels, and why he chose at the beginning of his literary career to write in English.

The strained and often abrupt endings of Conrad's novels may be the result of his need to put things in order, to follow in the tradition of the well-made novel. After asking so many questions, Conrad may have felt he must provide, if not absolute answers, at least firm direction. Perhaps it may be an inheritance—certainly it can be used as a rationalization—from a writer whom Conrad read in his uncle's library and a copy of whose work he carried with him for twenty years while at sea. Conrad's love of Shakespeare and his tribute to him is found throughout his work, in direct reference, in allusion, and in adaptation of Shakespearean scenes and characters. Shakespeare's fifth acts are a form of bringing together the disparate and opposing elements; the climax has passed, but not the resolution. If Conrad's conclusions lack power, it is not that he stayed with his characters and events after the climax of narration, but that he failed to invest the same craftsmanship and technical control over the material that he had applied earlier in his work. Conrad knew what had to be done; he had plans, great plans as Kurtz might have said. For whatever mysterious reason, he was unable to summon the technical resources adequate to meet the demands of literary resolution.

In his memoirs Conrad wrote of that moment when he decided to become a British seaman. While Conrad is explicit about this decision, he never states clearly why he chose to write in English. On the surface, the answer may seem obvious: he was a British seaman, a naturalized British citizen, a resident in England when not at sea. Why not then commit oneself fully in his work to an English identity? It was one way to heal the split in allegiance under which he was suffering, to leave behind his Polish past and devote himself fully to his new homeland. Possibly, too, Conrad, with his strong sense of the inevitable, knew intuitively he had to write in English because on the day he began *Almayer's Folly*, without any premeditation about the schedule, he was in an English boarding house, having just finished an English breakfast. To a man who operates on knowledge based on hints from the universe, such a manner of deciding things would not be considered unwise. Conrad's heroes made decisions that affected their lives on similar bases of evidence and coincidence.

There may still be another reason for Conrad's choice of English as his literary medium. As a foreigner, a man from a different land—an exile, even though a citizen—Conrad could see his new land and language from the perspective of an outsider. Native-born writers, he may have believed, are too close to their language; they cannot stand back and view it from a distance. A man not born into the language but one consciously adapting himself to it becomes more aware of its rules and curious irregularities; he does not have habit on which to rely.

Sitting in his study in his house in Canterbury at the end of his life, Conrad may have thought that he had, through his long labors, achieved perspective not only through esthetic distance but through linguistic distance as well. His best work was always seen in the recollection of action, not in the immediacy of the present tense of action. Somehow on the day he chose to write in English, he may have known that the "distance" he needed esthetically and spiritually lay partly in his choice of the language he knew third best at that time.

Bibliography

1. WORKS BY JOSEPH CONRAD

Almayer's Folly, novel. London: Unwin, 1895. New York: Macmillan, 1895.

An Outcast of the Islands, novel. London: Unwin, 1896. New York: Appleton, 1896.

The Nigger of the "Narcissus," novella. London: Heinemann, 1897, but dated "1898." Published in New York as *The Children of the Sea*, by Dodd, Mead, 1897.

Tales of Unrest, stories. New York: Scribners, 1898. London: Unwin, 1898. Contains "The Idiots," 1896; "Karain," 1897; "The Lagoon," 1897; "An Outpost of Progress," 1897; "The Return," 1898.

Lord Jim, novel. Edinburgh: Blackwood, 1900. New York: Doubleday, 1900.

The Inheritors (with Ford Madox Ford), novel. New York: McClure, Phillips, 1901. London: Heinemann, 1901.

Typhoon, novella. New York: Putnam's, 1902. Published in London as *Typhoon, and Other Stories* by Heinemann, 1903. London edition contains "Amy Foster," 1901; "Typhoon," 1902; "To-morrow," 1902; "Falk," 1903.

Youth: A Narrative and Two Other Stories, stories. Edinburgh: Blackwood, 1902. New York: McClure, Phillips, 1903.

Falk, Amy Foster, To-Morrow, stories. New York: McClure, Phillips, 1903.

Romance (with Ford Madox Ford), novel. London: Smith, Elder, 1903. New York: McClure, Phillips, 1904.

Nostromo, A Tale of the Seaboard, novel. London and New York: Harper, 1904.

The Mirror of the Sea, reminiscences. London: Methuen, 1906. New York: Harper, 1906.

The Secret Agent, A Simple Tale, novel. London: Methuen, 1907. New York: Harper, 1907.

Some Reminiscences, memoirs. Published serially in England, December 1908 to June 1909. Published in London in book form by Nash, 1912. Published in New York as *A Personal Record* by Harper, 1912.

A Set of Six, stories. London: Methuen, 1908. New York: Doubleday, Page, 1915. Contains "An Anarchist," 1906; "The Brute," 1906; "Gaspar Ruiz," 1906; "The Informer," 1906; "The Duel," 1908; "Il Conde," 1908.

Under Western Eyes, novel. London: Methuen, 1911. New York: Harper, 1911.

'Twixt Land and Sea: Tales. London: Dent, 1912. New York: G. H. Doran, 1912.

One Day More, a play in one act. London: *English Review*, 1913. (Adaptation of "To-morrow").

Chance, A Tale in Two Parts, novel. Published serially in New York Herald, 1913. London: Methuen, 1914. New York: Doubleday, Page, 1914.

Victory, An Island Tale, novel. New York: Doubleday, Page, 1915. London: Methuen, 1915.

Within the Tides, stories. London, 1915. New York: Doubleday, Page, 1916. Contains "The Partner," 1911; "The Inn of the Two Witches," 1913; "Because of the Dollars," 1914; "The Planter of Malata," 1914.

The Shadow-Line, A Confession, novella. London: Dent, 1917. New York: Doubleday, Page, 1917.

The Arrow of Gold, A Story Between Two Notes, novel. New York: Doubleday, Page, 1919. London: Unwin, 1919.

The Rescue, A Romance of the Shallows, novel. New York: Doubleday, Page, 1920. London: Dent, 1920.

Notes on Life and Letters, critical essays. London: Dent, 1921. New York: Doubleday, Page, 1921.

Notes on My Books, introductions and prefaces. New York: Doubleday, 1921. London: Heinemann, 1921.

The Works of Joseph Conrad, 20 vols. London: Heinemann, 1921–27.

The Secret Agent, Drama in Four Acts. Canterbury, 1921. (Adaptation of the novel.)

The Rover, novel. New York: Doubleday, Page, 1923. London: Unwin, 1923.

The Works of Joseph Conrad. The Uniform Edition, 22 vols. London: Dent, 1923–28. Reprinted as *Collected Edition of the Works of Joseph Conrad,* 21 vols., without the dramas. London: Dent, 1946–55.

Laughing Anne, and One Day More, two plays. London: Castle, 1924. New York: Doubleday, Page, 1925.

The Nature of a Crime (with Ford Madox Ford), novel. London: Duckworth, 1924. New York: Doubleday, Page, 1924.

Suspense, A Napoleonic Novel, unfinished novel. New York: Doubleday, Page, 1925. London: Dent, 1925.

Tales of Hearsay, stories. London: Unwin, 1925. New York: Doubleday, 1925. Contains "The Black Mate," 1908; "Prince Roman," 1911; "The Tale," 1917; "The Warrior's Soul," 1917.

Last Essays, collection of essays. London: Dent, 1926. New York: Doubleday, Page, 1926. Contains, among others, "The 'Torrens'," 1923; "The Congo Diary," 1925; "John Galsworthy," 1926.

The Sisters, fragment of novel. New York: Bookman Associates, 1928. New edition, 1970, by Mursia, in Milan, distributed by Parkers of Oxford, England.

Among valuable collections of letters are G. Jean-Aubry, *Joseph Conrad: Life and Letters,* 2 vols., published by Doubleday, Page in Garden City, N.Y. in 1927, and in London by Heinemann, 1927; G. Jean-Aubry, ed., *Joseph Conrad: Lettres Françaises,* published by Gallimard in Paris, 1929; Richard Curle, ed., *Conrad to a Friend: 150 Selected Letters from Joseph Conrad to Richard Curle,* Garden City: Doubleday, and London: Sampson, Low,

Marston, 1928; Edward Garnett, ed., *Letters from Joseph Conrad, 1895–1924*, published by Bobbs-Merrill, Indianapolis, 1928; John A. Gee and Paul J. Sturm, eds., *Letters of Joseph Conrad to Marguerite Poradowska, 1890–1920*, published by Yale University Press in New Haven, 1940; William Blackburn, ed., *Joseph Conrad: Letters to William Blackwood and David S. Meldrum*, published by Duke University Press in Durham, North Carolina, in 1958; Zdzislaw Najder, ed., *Conrad's Polish Background: Letters to and from Polish Friends*, published by Oxford University Press in London, 1963; C. T. Watts, ed., *Joseph Conrad's Letters to R. B. Cunninghame-Graham*, published by Cambridge University Press in London, 1969.

2. BOOKS ABOUT JOSEPH CONRAD

For detailed, complete bibliographies see Bruce E. Teets and Helmut E. Gerber, eds., *Joseph Conrad: An Annotated Bibliography of Writings about Him* (De Kalb, Ill.: Northern Illinois University Press, 1971); and Theodore G. Ehrsam, ed., *Bibliography of Joseph Conrad* (Metuchen, N.J.: Scarecrow Press, 1969). Earlier bibliographies of significant value are K. A. Lohf and E. P. Sheehy, eds., *Joseph Conrad at Mid-Century: Editions and Studies, 1895–1955* (Minneapolis: University of Minnesota Press, 1959); G. T. Keating, *A Conrad Memorial Library* (Garden City, N.Y.: Doubleday, Doran, 1929), with "Check-list of Additions," 1938; T. J. Wise, *A Bibliography of the Writings of Joseph Conrad, 1895–1921* (privately printed). See also *Modern Fiction Studies*, I (1955), which is devoted to Joseph Conrad studies.

The standard biography of Conrad is Jocelyn Baines, *Joseph Conrad: A Critical Biography*, published by Weidenfeld and Nicolson in London in 1960 and by McGraw-Hill in New York in 1960. Earlier full biographies are G. Jean-Aubry, *Joseph Conrad: Life and Letters*, 2 vols., published by Heinemann in London and Doubleday, Page in Garden City, N.Y., in 1927; G. Jean-Aubry's condensation of his earlier two-volume work into what he called the "definitive biography," *The Sea Dreamer*, published in 1957 by Doubleday, in a translation by Helen Sebba, and in London by Allen and Unwin, 1957; Jerry Allen's *The Thunder and the Sunshine*, published in 1958 by Doubleday. Jerry Allen also published a more specialized work, *The Sea Years of Joseph Conrad* in a 1965 Doubleday edition.

Some first-hand biographical studies and memoirs are by Jessie Conrad (Conrad's wife), *Joseph Conrad As I Knew Him* (London: Heinemann; Garden City, N.Y.: Doubleday, Page, 1926); and *Joseph Conrad and His Circle* (London: Jarrolds; New York: Dutton, 1935); Richard Curle, *The Last Twelve Years of Joseph Conrad* (London: Sampson, Low, Marston, 1928; New York: Doubleday, Doran, 1928); Ford Madox Ford, *Joseph Conrad: A Personal Remembrance* (Boston: Little, Brown, 1924); "Reminiscences of Conrad," by John Galsworthy in his *Castles in Spain and Other Screeds* (New York: Scribner's, 1927), pp. 99–126; and Borys Conrad's *My Father: Joseph Conrad* (London: Calder and Boyars, 1970).

A specialized interpretation is provided by Bernard C. Meyer, M.D., in his *Joseph Conrad: A Psychoanalytic Biography*, published by Princeton University Press in 1967.

Andreas, Osborn. *Joseph Conrad: A Study in Non-Conformity*. New York: Philosophical Library, 1949; London: Vision, 1962.

Bradbrook, M. C. *Joseph Conrad: Poland's English Genius*. Cambridge, Eng.: Cambridge University Press, 1941. Reprinted New York: Russell and Russell, 1965.

Cox, C. B. *Joseph Conrad: The Modern Imagination*. London: Dent, 1974.

Crankshaw, Edward. *Joseph Conrad: Some Aspects of the Art of the Novel*. London: John Lane, 1936.

Fleishman, Avrom. *Conrad's Politics*. Baltimore: Johns Hopkins University Press, 1967.

Gillon, Adam. *The Eternal Solitary: A Study of Joseph Conrad*. New York: Bookman Associates, 1960.

Gordon, John Dozier. *Joseph Conrad: The Making of a Novelist*. Cambridge, Mass.: Harvard University Press, 1941.

Graver, Lawrence. *Conrad's Short Fiction*. Berkeley, Calif.: University of California Press, 1969.

Guerard, Albert J. *Conrad the Novelist*. Cambridge, Mass.: Harvard University Press, 1958.

————. *Joseph Conrad*. New York: New Directions, 1947.

Gurko, Leo. *Joseph Conrad: Giant in Exile*. New York: Macmillan, 1962.

Haugh, Robert E. *Joseph Conrad: Discovery in Design*. Norman, Oklahoma: University of Oklahoma Press, 1957.

Hay, Eloise Knapp. *The Political Novels of Joseph Conrad*. Chicago: University of Chicago Press, 1963.

Hewitt, Douglas. *Conrad: A Reassessment*. Cambridge, Eng.: Bowes and Bowes, 1952.

Johnson, Bruce. *Conrad's Models of Mind*. Minneapolis: University of Minnesota Press, 1971.

Hoffman, Stanton De Voren. *Comedy and Form in the Fiction of Joseph Conrad*. The Hague: Mouton, 1970.

Kirschner, Paul. *Conrad: The Psychologist as Artist*. Edinburgh: Oliver and Boyd, 1968.

Lee, Robert E. *Conrad's Colonialism*. The Hague: Mouton, 1970.

Megroz, R. L. *Conrad's Mind and Method: A Study of Personality in Art*. London: Faber and Faber, 1931.

Morf, Gustav. *The Polish Heritage of Joseph Conrad*. London: Sampson, Low, Marston, 1930; New York: Smith, 1930.

Moser, Thomas. *Joseph Conrad: Achievement and Decline*. Cambridge, Mass.: Harvard University Press, 1957.

Palmer, John A. *Joseph Conrad's Fiction: A Study in Literary Growth*. Ithaca, N.Y.: Cornell University Press, 1968.

Rosenfield, Claire. *Paradise of Snakes*. Chicago: University of Chicago Press, 1967.

Roussel, Royal. *The Metaphysics of Darkness*. Baltimore: Johns Hopkins University Press, 1971.

Said, Edward. *Joseph Conrad and the Fiction of Autobiog-*

raphy. Cambridge, Mass.: Harvard University Press, 1966.

Sherry, Norman. *Conrad's Western World*. Cambridge, Eng.: Cambridge University Press, 1971.

————. *Conrad's Eastern World*. Cambridge, Eng.: Cambridge University Press, 1966.

Stewart, J. I. M. *Joseph Conrad*. New York: Dodd, Mead, 1968.

Wiley, Paul. *Conrad's Measure of Man*. Madison, Wisc.: University of Wisconsin Press, 1954.

Wright, Walter F. *Romance and Tragedy in Joseph Conrad*. Lincoln, Nebr.: University of Nebraska Press, 1949.

3.   ARTICLES ON JOSEPH CONRAD

Allen, Walter. *The English Novel*. New York: E. P. Dutton, 1954, pp. 361–74.

Bernard, Kenneth. "Conrad's Fools of Innocence in *The Nigger of the Narcissus*," *Conradiana*, II, No. 1 (Fall 1969–70), 49–58.

Brown, Douglas. "From *Heart of Darkness* to *Nostromo*: An Approach to Conrad," in Boris Ford, ed., *The Modern Age*, Pelican Guide to English Literature, VII (Baltimore: Penguin Books, 1961), 119–37.

Crews, Frederick C. "The Power of *Darkness*," *Partisan Review*, XXXIV, No. 4 (Fall, 1967), 507–25.

Curle, Richard. "Conrad's Diary," *Yale Review*, XV (January, 1926), 254–66.

Day, Robert A. "The Rebirth of Leggatt," *Literature and Psychology*, XIII (Summer 1963), 74–80.

Dike, Donald A. "The Tempest of Axel Heyst," *Nineteenth-Century Fiction*, XVII (September 1962), 95–113.

Evans, Robert O. "Conrad's Underworld," *Modern Fiction Studies*, II (May 1956), 56–62.

Forster, E. M. *Abinger Harvest*. New York: Harcourt Brace, 1936, pp. 136–41.

Harkness, Bruce, ed. *Conrad's Secret Sharer and the Critics*. Belmont, Calif.: Wadsworth, 1962.

Harper, George M. "Conrad's Knitters and Homer's Cave of the Nymphs," *English Language Notes*, I (September 1963), 53–57.

Holland, Norman N. "Style as Character: *The Secret Agent*," *Modern Fiction Studies*, XII (Summer, 1966), 221–31.

Howe, Irving. "Conrad: Order and Anarchy," in his *Politics and the Novel*. New York: Horizon Press and Meridian Books, 1957, pp. 76–113.

James, Henry. "The New Novel, 1914," in his *Notes on Novelists*. New York: Scribner's, pp. 314–61.

Karl, Frederick and Marvin Magalaner. *A Reader's Guide to Great Twentieth Century English Novels*. New York: Noonday Press, 1959, pp. 42–99.

Kettle, Arnold. "The Greatness of Joseph Conrad," *Modern Quarterly*, III (Summer 1948), 64–70.

Kimbrough, Robert, ed. *Heart of Darkness: Text, Sources, Criticism*. New York: Norton, 1963.

Krieger, Murray. "Joseph Conrad: Action, Inaction, and Extremity," in his *The Tragic Vision*. New York: Holt, 1960, pp. 154–94.

Krzyzanowski, Ludwik, ed. *Joseph Conrad: Centennial Essays*. New York: Polish Institute of Arts and Sciences in America.

Leavis, F. R. "Joseph Conrad," in his *The Great Tradition: George Eliot, Henry James, Joseph Conrad*. New York: George W. Stewart; London: Chatto and Windus, 1948, pp. 173–226.

Leiter, Louis H. "Echo Structures: Conrad's 'The Secret Sharer,'" *Twentieth-Century Literature*, V (January 1960), 159–75.

Masefield, John. "Deep Sea Yarns: Youth, a Narrative," *Speaker*, XXXIV (January 31, 1903), 20–24.

Miller, J. Hillis. *Poets of Reality: Six Twentieth-Century Writers*. Cambridge, Mass.: Belknap Press, 1965, pp. 13–67.

Morris, Robert L. "The Classical Reference in Conrad's Fiction," *College English*, VII (March 1946), 312–18.

Moynihan, William T. "Conrad's 'The End of the Tether':
    A New Reading," *Modern Fiction Studies*, IX (Win-
    ter 1963–64), 390–93.

Mudrick, Marvin, ed. *Conrad: A Collection of Critical
    Essays*. Englewood Cliffs, N.J.: Prentice-Hall, 1966.

Owen, Guy. "Crane's 'The Open Boat' and Conrad's
    'Youth,' " *Renascence*, XVI Fall 1963, 22–28.

Ryf, Robert S. "Conrad's Stage *Victory*," *Modern Drama*,
    VII (September 1964), 148–60.

Spector, Robert Donald. "Irony as Theme: Conrad's *The
    Secret Agent*," *Nineteenth-Century Fiction*, XII (June
    1958), 69–71.

Stallman, Robert W., ed. *The Art of Joseph Conrad: A
    Critical Symposium*. East Lansing, Mich.: Michigan
    State University Press, 1960.

————. "Conrad Criticism Today," *Sewanee Review*,
    LXVII (Winter 1959), 135–45.

Stein, William Bysshe. "Buddhism and 'Heart of Dark-
    ness,' " *Western Humanities Review*, XI (Summer
    1957), 281–85.

Stewart, J. I. M. Eight Modern Writers, Vol. XII of *Ox-
    ford History of English Literature* (Oxford: Clarendon
    Press, 1963), pp. 184–222.

Tanner, Tony. "Butterflies and Beetles—Conrad's Two
    Truths," *Chicago Review*, XVI (Winter–Spring
    1963), 123–40.

————. "Nightmare and Complacency: Razumov and the
    Western Eye," *Critical Quarterly*, IV (Autumn 1962),
    197–214.

Tillyard, E. M. W. "*The Secret Agent* Reconsidered,"
    Essays in Criticism, XI (July 1961), 309–18.

Tindall, W. Y. "Apology for Marlow," in R. C. Rathburn
    and M. Steinmann Jr., eds., *From Jane Austen to Jo-
    seph Conrad*. Minneapolis: University of Minnesota
    Press, 1959.

Van Ghent, Dorothy. "On *Lord Jim*," in her *The English
    Novel: Form and Function*. New York: Rinehart,
    1953, pp. 229–44.

Warner, Oliver; John Wain; W. W. Robson; Richard
    Freislich; Tom Hopkinson; Jocelyn Baines; Richard

Curle: "Joseph Conrad: A Critical Symposium," *London* magazine, IV (November 1957), 21–49.

Warren, Robert Penn. Introduction to *Nostromo*. New York: Modern Library, 1951. Reprinted from *Sewanee Review*, LIX (Summer 1951), 363–91.

Watt, Ian. "Joseph Conrad: Alienation and Commitment," in H. S. Davies and George Watson, eds., *The English Mind*. Cambridge, Eng.: Cambridge University Press, 1946, pp. 257–78.

Young, Vernon. "Joseph Conrad: Outline for a Reconsideration," *Hudson Review*, II (Spring 1949), 5–19.

Zabel, Morton David. "Conrad," in his *Craft and Character in Modern Fiction*. New York: Viking, 1957, pp. 147–227. Includes revised version of "Joseph Conrad: Chance and Recognition," *Sewanee Review*, LIII (Winter 1945), 1–22.

Index

MODERN LITERATURE MONOGRAPHS

In the same series (continued from page ii)